1970

His presence in the world

His presence
in the world

A study of eucharistic worship
and theology

Nicholas Lash

Pflaum Press  Dayton, Ohio 1968

First published 1968

Nihil obstat: John Coventry SJ, Censor
Imprimatur: ✠ Patrick Casey, Vicar-General
Westminster, 22 November 1967

The Nihil obstat and Imprimatur are a declaration that
a book or pamphlet is considered to be free from
doctrinal or moral error. It is not implied that those who
have granted the Nihil obstat and Imprimatur agree
with the contents, opinions, or statements expressed.

Library of Congress Catalog Card Number 68-22896

Printed in the United States of America

to David Woodard
parish priest
from his curate

Contents

Foreword

To say that the celebration of the eucharist is central to the faith and life of the christian people is not to say anything very original. But neither is it the end of the matter. Precisely because the eucharist is so central, the many questions that are currently being raised about every aspect of our christian existence are all, in one way or another, questions which illuminate our search for a deeper understanding of the eucharist. In this book, therefore, I have tried to approach the problem of the eucharist from a number of different points of view, each of which should help to add depth to the others. If, by thus expressing some aspects of my own very limited understanding of the *mysterium fidei*, I shall have helped anybody else to deepen, and to express, their own understanding of the same mystery, I shall have done all that I set out to do.

I would like to express my gratitude to the editors of *The Clergy Review* and *New Blackfriars*, in which chapters 2 and 5 first appeared, and to the editor of *Tijdschrift voor Theologie*, in which chapter 6 first appeared (in Dutch). In the first two cases, I have made a number of small alterations, mostly in the interests of clarity.

Nicholas Lash

Slough, 23 September 1967

1
What on earth is theology?

In a recent book Cardinal Heenan wrote that: 'The word dialogue has created barriers between people. To propose a dialogue is to assume that easy familiar conversation has become impossible.'[1] There is a measure of truth in this, but it is perhaps more accurate to say that the technical meaning which the word *dialogue* has recently acquired draws attention to the fact that the assumption of agreement between people, the assumption of a common viewpoint, is the best of all possible barriers to effective mutual communication. Because just such an assumption is prevalent amongst English catholics, the task of the theologian is made more than usually difficult. As theology probes, enquires, develops, rethinks its method and presuppositions as well as its terminology, the things that theologians say are often irreconcilable with this assumption of a common viewpoint, shared on all topics by all catholics. But, precisely

[1] *Council and Clergy* (London 1966) 101.

because the assumption persists, unexamined, the only possible reaction, very often, is to question the motives and 'catholic integrity' of the theologian.[2] It would therefore seem necessary, before particular doctrinal issues can be discussed with any serenity, to examine more fundamental questions concerning the nature, function, and method of theology. Here the theologian, at least in English-speaking lands, is up against another difficulty. Fundamental questions can usually only be formulated in rather abstract terms, and we English, who pride ourselves on a healthy anti-intellectualism, immediately suspect that the man who trades in abstractions is himself abstracted from the concrete agony of birth and death, peace and war, brotherhood and despair.

Much of this book is devoted to a discussion of the eucharist, and the celebration of the eucharist, a gathering of people in one place to do something quite specific, is clearly not at all an abstract affair. Any discussion of the eucharist, however, necessarily presupposes that certain basic questions concerning the nature of christian belief and commitment have already been examined. Much of the irrelevance and ineffectiveness of christianity in the modern world can be traced to a failure, on the part of christians, to ask the right questions about the relationship of their christian belief to this world in which they live. The reason, therefore, why this chapter is entitled: 'What on earth is theology?', is that if we have not grasped what theology is saying about this world, if we do not understand what theology is on *earth*, we shall

[2] The reader should, without difficulty, be able to illustrate this contention from his own experience.

not be likely to devote any of our limited time on earth
to doing theology.

Even those people (and they do exist) who suspect that
theology is irrelevant to the business of practical living
could hardly deny that the 'problem of God' is not only
felt by many people to be acutely real, but is currently
taking on a sharply new form.[3] We can hardly afford to
ignore the fact that much contemporary christian discussion is centred on the possibility of what is sometimes
referred to as 'religionless christianity' and on the assertion that 'God is dead' (which may be either a lament or
a cry of liberation), and that we have to construct a
theology without him. There is no God, as one wag put
it, and Jesus is his son. The problem of God is *man*'s
problem of God, and the contemporary form of the
problem invites us to ask at least, in all seriousness, the
question: 'Is christianity (and so theology, since christian
theology is the articulation of christian belief) about
God or about man?' The apparently easy answer to that
question is that it is about both. The heart and centre
of the christian message concerns the humanisation (or
incarnation) of God, the purpose of which is, within the
limits of the possible, the divinisation of man. Jesus
Christ is, according to the Council of Chalcedon, *verus
Deus et verus homo*. Both God and man; but, as we shall
see, this does not solve the problem.

Much recent and contemporary atheism owes its
dynamism to the conviction that to admit the existence
of God is necessarily to restrict the possibility of human

[3] Cf John Courtney Murray, 'On the Structure of the Problem
of God', in *Theological Studies* (Baltimore) XXIII (1962) 1–26.

freedom and fulfilment. If God exists, is not the genuine
freedom of humanity reduced by the fact of God, and by
the fact that he has, apparently, made certain claims
upon man: 'Eat of this fruit and you shall most surely
die.' An elderly and devout anglican lady once said to
me that she sometimes feels like a butterfly stuck with
a pin. Is she the only christian who has ever had that
feeling? Incidentally, it is small consolation to say to the
butterfly: 'It is in your own deepest interests to be stuck
with a pin.'

Another illustration of this dilemma can be found in
the rather glib way in which christians sometimes talk
as if they had two distinct commandments to fulfil, the
love of God and the love of the brethren, and that the
fulfilling of each commandment occupied distinct areas
of their time and energy. At our best, we talk as if these
two loves could conflict (which, if it were true, would
prove the atheist's point that the existence of God restricted human fulfilment). At our worst, we talk as if
formal prayer was 'loving God', and sticking elastoplast
on the knees of a screaming child was 'loving our
brother'. Then we spend a great deal of time discussing
how each of these two apparently contradictory commandments can be fulfilled without detriment to the
other (we call this the 'prayer and good works' con-
troversy). So far as I know, nobody has ever actually
said: 'Excuse me, brother, I can't love you at the
moment; I'm too busy loving God'; but, in the framework of the discussion, the seeds are sown of even this
interesting possibility.

It therefore becomes clear that the real difficulty in
saying that christianity, or theology, is about both God

and man, the real difficulty in *verus Deus et verus homo,* consists not in knowing what we mean by *God* or what we mean by *man* (though these are not small questions), but in the difficulty of knowing what we mean by *and.* There does not seem to be room for both of us. Either God exists, in which case man's space for living and developing freely is limited; or man is free, and God must go. If we are going to make any sense of our christian belief, a belief in the God and Father of our Lord Jesus Christ, then we have to be clear that the Council of Chalcedon was declaring our faith, affirming our problem, not solving it. The council was not saying that Jesus is God plus man; that he is partly God and partly man; but that he is totally divine and totally human. Christianity is not a new religion (loving God), from which flows a new morality (loving the brother). Christianity is unique precisely in its affirmation that, in Christ, the religious and the moral are identified; that, in Christ, human concern and human relationships are the disclosure of God; that, in Christ, God comes to be in humanity in the measure that humanity is opened to his limitless transcendence. The human possibility becomes, in Christ, the (human) possibility of God.[4] If in the past we have often understood the *et* of *verus Deus*

[4] After drafting this chapter, I came across Gabriel Moran's important book *The Theology of Revelation* (London 1967), in which all the things I have tried to say in this chapter are considerably better said. In the present context, Moran says: 'In a world seeking freedom by the establishment of private autonomy, Jesus is the unsurpassable testimony that not only is freedom not destroyed by proximity to God, but that man is free precisely insofar as he is present to God. Jesus is the living proof that man is freedom for God' (160).

et verus homo as additive, if we have made God into 'a'
being, who can be set alongside other beings, who can
compete with them for our attention, and so on, then
this concept of God must go.

In primitive religion it seems that there does tend
to be this conflict between God and man, between the
demands of the divine and the demands of the human.
In the old testament a moving example of this tension
(an example that is moving precisely because it shows
the first glimmer of light, the light that will dissolve
the dark tension) is the story of Abraham and Isaac.
Abraham, whose initial insights are those of his own
religious culture, sorrowfully concludes that fidelity to
God entails the betrayal of his son. In the act of betraying his son, the realisation explodes that the freedom of
his son is the expression of his fidelity to God. The
fathers of the church were not wrong to see in this in-
cident the first tentative sketch of that definitive can-
cellation of 'God-as-a-rival-being' in which the human
flourishing of the resurrection would spring, from the
betrayal of the Son, as the achievment of fidelity to God.
In this sense, as the exorcism of primitive religion,
christianity is about the 'death' of God, the death of the
'gods', and christianity is a profoundly irreligious business. Let us say that christianity is about the liberating
humanisation of God ('liberating humanisation', by the
way, is an attempt to translate 'redemptive incarnation'
into English). But in the enfleshment of God's word it is
not God who is liberated, but man. God is eternal freedom; by plunging himself into the dark unfreedom of

our human misery, by exploding our death into his life, he has set us free. What Calvary, Easter, and the sending of the Spirit say is that now we can be human, now we can begin to breathe—with his Spirit—now we can love, now we can be brothers. The butterfly was on the pin before; now the butterfly has before it the possibility of spreading its wings and flying.

The fact that, in that last paragraph, I was forced into metaphor indicates that, once one has accepted that christianity is indeed about both God and man, but that one is using *and* in a rather queer way, then it becomes very difficult to talk about christianity. With the realisation of what christianity is about (and what it is not about), theology, as the articulation of belief in human brotherhood made newly possible in a love and freedom that is of God, itself becomes possible—but not easy. Later in this chapter, I shall try to suggest in rather more detail what is involved in a profession of faith in the divinity of the man Jesus. Before doing so, however, there is one rather different question that must be raised.

I am not quite sure how this next question should be formulated. It could go: Is theology an individual or a collective project?; or, Is theology a personal or a public project?; or, Is theology a subjective or an objective project? Now although I am no philosopher, it is obvious, even to me, that those are the sorts of question which no well-educated man would ask, any more than he would ask: 'Have you stopped beating your wife?' However, it is sometimes true that the best way of getting at the right question is to ask the wrong one, especially when, as is the case with catholic theology, the wrong question has so often been presumed to be not only correct but obviously correct.[5]

In recent catholic tradition, theology, the articulation of belief, has for a long time been handled as an almost exclusively collective or public project. The good news of Jesus Christ, as it reaches most of us, takes the form of an immensely complex system of abstract propositions, which system is called theology. I am not, I think, being simply anachronistic or troublesome if I say that I cannot imagine St Peter, in answer to the crowd's question at Pentecost: 'What must we do brothers?', saying: 'I have a book in my pocket; go away and study it'. And yet we have come to regard theology as something already available, out there on the table, which people must learn. The pupil in a catholic school learns a simplified, skeletal version of the 'thing', in rather the same way as he learns the twelve-times table, or the principal natural resources of the Indian sub-continent. The trainee teacher learns a somewhat fuller version, and the poor student priest has to assimilate the entire conceptual juggernaut. This is a caricature, of course, especially in these days of catechetical and seminary reform, but it is sufficiently close to the truth to raise some rather awkward questions about the way in which, at least until very recently, we understood the process of transmission and reception of God's revelation.

[5] 'The history of theories of revelation is not the history of subjectivists and objectivists, but the history of those who tried to steer a middle course, and much to their dismay found themselves accused of one or the other. It might be that this has continually happened not because the middle way was not carefully steered, but because the middle way does not exist ... "there is no mean between two errors" ' (Moran, 172).

Under these conditions, it is hardly surprising that the verbal witness to Christ on the part of the ordinary catholic is often muted. He is nervous about discussing his faith with his friends, because he is acutely aware of the fact that theology is 'above his head', and he does not want to let the side down. While such a person's belief is often both unified and profound, it is a little dangerous to assume, as is sometimes done by those in positions of ecclesiastical authority, that 'simplicity' of faith increases in direct proportion to a man's inability to articulate his belief.[6]

It is not, however, only the lay person's witness which is adversely affected by this state of affairs. If 'learning theology' is conceived of as a process similar to learning the data in a geography text-book, teaching theology is conceived of on the same pattern. The *traditio fidei* becomes, not 'sharing faith', but something known as 'handing on *the* faith' (there it is, out there on the table, in the book), and, at least until the second Vatican Council, the apostolic teaching office of a bishop often seemed to consist not so much in bearing effective witness to belief in concrete situations as in the repetition of ready-made propositions.[7] The principal danger in

[6] Certainty and understanding are, however closely related, distinct mental states (or, to use Bernard Lonergan's terminology, judgement and insight are distinct mental acts). Those who try to exalt the virtue of faith (which, intellectually, is in the order of certainty) by depreciating the importance of the search for understanding (the *fides quaerens intellectum*), have confused the two (cf Bernard Lonergan *Insight* London 1958).

[7] 'Revelation is not a thing, an object that can be placed somewhere and kept intact. Revelation is what happens between persons and exists only as a personal reality. If there is revelation

conceiving of theology in this way is that it ceases to be a witness to belief on anybody's part (and so a bishop can say that if, on a crucial issue, the pope suddenly changes his mind, then the bishop will, without any difficulty, immediately change his mind too). The propositions have become divorced from the minds of men, and the test of orthodoxy is no longer what a man believes, but what he says.

To put the point slightly differently, theology, as divorced from belief, becomes talking about somebody else's idea of God. Teaching theology means getting one person to accept another person's understanding of God. Since very often it is not, for either teacher or pupil, their own understanding of God that is involved, theology ceases to be discourse about God, the living God, at all.[8]

Now, still accepting the wrong question with which I began, the wife-beating question, let us see what happens if we opt for the alternative: for an individual, or personal, or subjective notion of theology. Each human being is not only unique, in a unique situation calling for a unique response, but there is, at the heart of each one of us, a loneliness, the overcoming of which is the work of our redemption, but which can only be completely overcome where it takes its origin, in death.

---

anywhere in the Church today, it can only be in the conscious experience of people' (Moran, 120).

[8] 'It is a regrettable but undeniable fact that indolent teachers and pastors have thought that they had automatically transmitted revelation because they had taught Christian doctrine and had had the creed memorised. But this is the fault neither of creed nor of doctrinal formulas, but of human beings' (Moran, 143).

Therefore, in the concrete, I can only believe what *I* believe. The articulation of my belief, which is my theology, cannot be identical, at all points, with anybody else's. If it is, then one of us is lying. Ultimately it is less important, surely, that a man talk according to the book than that he declare, with an honesty of which few of us are capable, the truth that is in him. The fact that a man is prepared to say all the right things does not adequately demonstrate that he is an orthodox believer; it does not in fact demonstrate that he believes anything at all.[9]

If this insistence that, since faith is an intensely personal thing, therefore theology must be an intensely personal thing, constituted all that there was to be said, then there would be no such thing as theology. A state of affairs in which the theological project broke down into the discordant babbling of individual believers incapable of mutual communication would be no more satisfactory than the state of affairs in which the whole well-drilled army dutifully repeated its uncomprehended catalogue of propositions concerning a God in whom few of them believed.

In the first section of this chapter it was suggested that christianity, and so theology, is only about God and man in the sense that it is about being human in a new

[9] 'If Christ is not understood to be *now* revealing God to man, faith is bound to become (despite our protests to the contrary) the rational acceptance of past facts and present teachings which are extrinsic to the sanctifying-worshipping activity now taking place. But belief is not directed to a message but to God raising up Christ, and this is not a past event but an ever present, continuing occurrence' (Moran, 116; that final phrase is not particularly happy, but the point he is making is, I think, clear).

way. It is about the recovery, and the discovery, of human brotherhood that springs from the love God has for us, poured into our hearts through Christ Jesus our Lord. Though we may necessarily objectify our ideas about God, it is of fundamental importance to affirm that God is not an object. We do not love God plus man: we love man with a love which is of God, we love our brother in God. We do not talk about God plus man: we talk about man with a knowledge which is of God, we know our brother in God.

In the next section we saw how hopeless it was to accept either horn of the proffered dilemma. Our discourse about God cannot only be the passing on, from hand to hand, of somebody else's belief in God. It cannot only be a matter of keeping our hands clean, so far as propositional orthodoxy is concerned. Equally, our discourse about God cannot only be the incommunicable articulation of our unique belief in God, as unique individuals. Not the least of the reasons for this is that God's revelation, his intelligible (if wholly mysterious) self-disclosure in human history, anticipates the encounter with it, and faithful acceptance of it, on the part of the individual.[10] To escape the dilemma, and to link

[10] On the part of all individuals other than the man Jesus. Cf Moran's chapter, 'Christ as Revelatory Communion', the programme for which he sets out as follows: 'In this chapter I wish rather to assert: (1) that God's revelation not only reaches a high point in Christ but is recapitulated in him; (2) that the participating subject who first receives the Christ-revelation is not the apostolic community but Christ himself; (3) that the fullness of revelation reached at the resurrection cannot perdure in books or institutions but only in the consciousness of the glorified Lord' (58).

these two sections together, I now propose to say something about the structure of christian belief.

Christian belief is born in the context of brotherhood.
The truth of this assertion, although it should be obvious to any student of the new testament, cannot by any means be taken for granted. For many people, 'belief in Jesus Christ' is taken to refer to a private compartment of their personal existence, although they would agree that the authenticity of this belief is to be measured by the love of the brother that should flow from it. But to say that christian belief is born in the context of brotherhood is to say something more than: 'I believe in Jesus, and I will love other people because he told us to.' It is to say that belief in Jesus is, directly and formally, a commitment to brotherhood.

This becomes a little clearer if we remember that the sacrament of baptism, the sealing of christian faith by that symbolic washing which denotes and achieves an involvement in the death of Jesus, is itself the rite by which a man is incorporated into the brotherhood of believers. It becomes clearer still if we glance at the content of our Lord's preaching.

By his preaching, Jesus was concerned to provoke in his hearers an immediate response to fundamental questions concerning their personal identity and integrity. Through his parables, especially, he was trying to force a decision by the listener as to where he stood, now, in regard to God's future kingdom.[11] God's future kingdom

[11] '. . . the parables are weapons of warfare. Everyone of them calls for an immediate response' (Joachim Jeremias *The Parables of Jesus* London 1963, 21).

will consist in that consummation of human brother-hood in which each individual will have become most fully himself because he will, with all the barriers down, be totally shared and sharing in the knowledge and love of God. The decision had to be made now because I can-not decide tomorrow whether I am going to risk the business of loving today. To postpone the decision is to refuse, today, to love.[12] Moreover, in the context of our Lord's preaching, it was a decision about the following of Jesus, the imitation of Christ. The reason for this is that Jesus presented himself as the man who, because he personally was totally open, totally exposed to that ultimate reality he called his Father, was prepared to risk anything, everything, for his brethren. We spend our time pathetically trying to hug to ourselves a tiny, circumscribed area of existence, the things we can understand and control, the people we think we can dominate. We push away, angrily, the things we cannot understand, the people we cannot dominate and, there-fore, dare not trust. Jesus was prepared to let go of all this, to release the circumscribed area of existence, to lose 'his' life.[13]

The disciple, in being called to a present commitment to the future kingdom, a present commitment to the construction of a brotherhood whose full achievement lies in the future, at the horizon of history, is being called to the same loss of 'his' life. To 'follow Jesus' is to

[12] Cf Karl Rahner, 'The "Commandment" of love in Relation to the Other Commandments', in *Theological Investigations* v (London 1966).

[13] Cf Sebastian Moore *God is a New Language* (London 1967). 122.

accept, in the gift of oneself, the relationship made possible by Jesus, in Jesus' own total self-gift to his brethren. But who is this man whose commitment to the human project rings with the unconditioned clarity of the absolute: this man who, in that commitment, constitutes and heralds a brotherhood which is similarly unconditioned? In asking this question we have, in fact, returned to the problem of what it means to say that Jesus is *verus Deus et verus homo*. To see how this is the case it may be helpful to try to follow the disciples in their growing understanding of Jesus, an understanding which culminated in the affirmation of his divinity. In other words, by trying to describe the context in which the apostolic church came to her final understanding of her Lord, we should be helped to make the discovery which she made, in a manner appropriate to our own situation.

Before considering what it could mean to attribute divinity to Jesus Christ, there is one important preliminary observation to be made: it concerns the 'naming of God'. We cannot name God. I think that we have to start from there. Any word used to signify the all-holy mystery that lies at the heart of and beyond created reality, is a totally inadequate symbol for the inexpressible. It would be as well, each time we are tempted to launch off into one of our facile descriptions of the almighty and his activity, whether in terms of the rich imagery of biblical thought, or in the taut, abstract categories of classical theology, to remind ourselves of St Thomas' stern insistence that we cannot know what God is. And if St Thomas does not happen to be congenial to our particular taste, we could read St John of the Cross or the *Cloud of Unknowing* instead. That way we might save ourselves from the host of false personal and theological problems that arise when we imply that God changes his mind, loses his temper, is a spectator (apparently impotent for all his omnipotence) to the suffering of the innocent, smiles benignly on our trivial attempts at self-improvement, and so on. When personally confronted with the all-holy mystery, the appropriate reaction of man is silent adoration.[14]

When, in the new testament, the term *ho theos* is used to designate the mystery, there is no question of its being used as the vocalisation of an idea which we all have and can bandy about in confident fashion. I am more and more persuaded that what is wrong with so much that passes for theology, ancient and modern, is its fundamental irreverence; its habit of using the term *God* as if it were a pawn, with a clearly defined conceptual content, in a game of intellectual chess.

In the new testament the term *ho theos* does not stand for an idea of divinity; it points beyond itself to the concrete, personal, all-holy, to the limitless origination that grounds our limited reality. In the new testa-

---

[14] And outside this context of personal, existential confrontation (a confrontation that may take the form of the experienced 'absence' of God), any discussion of the 'existence' or 'meaning' of God can only be a false statement of the problem. Any discussion of the possibility, necessity, or value of 'natural' theology lies outside the scope of this chapter. As a matter of theological method, however, it is important to stress that a 'proof' of God, the attempt to arrive at a theoretical judgement, prior to any experience of him, 'that God exists', is a rejection of the whole biblical and patristic tradition. In this tradition the experience of God in his salvific activity (or in its apparent absence) is prior to all conceptualisation concerning the mystery. Cf Moran, 163–4; John Courtney Murray, 1–26.

ment the term *ho theos* does not indicate an idea, but a person, that person whom we are tremblingly privileged to call our Father. There is, therefore, no question of saying simply that Jesus is *ho theos*. Each of us is conscious, in the measure that he is humanly and religiously awakened, of his relationship to the unnameable mystery of origination, our origination, our Father. Our search for words to use about Christ's unique relationship to the mystery can hardly go beyond the statement that he is, uniquely, the *huios tou theou*, the Son of the Father.[15]

One quite often hears catholics say: 'But how can we enter into ecumenical discussion with other christians? Some of them don't even believe in the divinity of Jesus.' I have never yet heard a catholic say: 'Some of them don't even believe in the humanity of God.' Perhaps it is because we tend not to ourselves. In *Honest to God*, Bishop Robinson wrote:

> ... popular ... Christology has always been dominantly docetic. That is to say, Christ only appeared to be a man or looked like a man: 'underneath' he was God ... even if such a view would be indignantly repudiated by orthodox Christians, and however much they would insist that Jesus was 'perfect man' as well as 'perfect God', still the traditional ... way of describing the Incarnation almost inevitably suggests that Jesus was really God walking about on earth, dressed up as a man.[16]

[15] Cf Karl Rahner, 'Theos in the New Testament', in *Theological Investigations* 1 (London 1961).

[16] 65–6. 'The idea that God disguises himself as a man, or that needing to make himself visible, he makes gestures by means of a human reality which is used in such a way that it is not a real

The point which Bishop Robinson is making can, perhaps, be focused more precisely by suggesting that many
people think of Jesus as physically human and psychologically divine. They are not surprised that 'he knew
what was in the heart of man': after all, he was God,
wasn't he? Is it not true that many catholics find it quite
easy to accept that Jesus knew what was going on in
other people's minds; they find it quite easy to accept
that he could foretell the day and manner of his death.
But they get distinctly uneasy if one talks of Jesus learning, Jesus worrying, Jesus being tempted. A rather
extreme example of this uneasiness is the case of a highly
educated and dedicated catholic who, in conversation a
couple of years ago, violently rejected the idea that Jesus
freely decided to accept the will of God. And yet, without that free human decision, that obedience, the cross
becomes a conjuring-trick, and the new testament a
fairy-tale.

I suggested earlier that only the discovery of the mystery that *I* am conscious of, that I adore, that I try to
talk about, stands any chance of escaping the charge of
idolatry. In other words, to put it rather crudely, any
discovery of God that comes simply from the 'outside'
(accepting somebody else's God) is not a discovery of
God at all.[17] The road to belief is not a process of acquir-

---

man with independence and freedom, but a puppet on strings
which the player behind the scenes uses to make himself audible
... is mythology and not Church dogma' (Karl Rahner *Theological Investigations* IV, London 1966, 118).

[17] 'Since revelation is the act of a participating subject becoming aware of his communion with God and man, it should be
obvious that such things as violence, social pressure, or mass

ing facility in manipulating the terms of religious discourse. It is the long, dark, painful road of exposure,
my exposure, to reality, my reality and the mystery
which grounds it.[18] And because, given the facts of the
human condition, reality runs right into death, the road
to God is a road to death, my death.

What can we say about Jesus' relationship to God? How
can we get beyond the *et* of *verus Deus et verus homo,*
and try to say something meaningful about Jesus' conscious relationship to his Father, about his conscious
exposure to the mystery?[19] The first thing to be said is
that we cannot inspect Jesus' consciousness, for the very
good reason that we cannot inspect anybody's consciousness. Our human discourse consists in trying, through

---

advertising techniques cannot be the means of communicating
revelation' (Moran, 154).

[18] Cf Michael Novak *Belief and Unbelief* (New York 1965).
This raises once again the whole question of what is meant by
'religious education'. The problem is not one of replacing
'abstract propositions' by 'concrete images' or 'salvation-history',
but of deciding whether God's revelation consists simply in past
events or whether it includes man's present response. 'The
poverty of our Christian instruction, and the poverty of our
common life, was at first thought to consist in the inadequacy of
the *content* of our teaching. The remedy was thought to lie in
"getting back to the Bible". It doesn't. It consists in getting back
to ourselves' (Sebastian Moore, 145).

[19] 'One of the most pressing needs of contemporary theology is
to work out a theology of Christ's consciousness and psychological development as a complement to the theology expressed
in the Chalcedonic categories' (Moran, 66). One theologian who
has made an important contribution here is Karl Rahner.
Another is Bernard Lonergan, and I was surprised to notice that,
although Moran is acquainted with Lonergan's work, he does not
refer to his important study *De Constitutione Christi Ontologica
et Psychologica* (Rome 1956).

the common tool of language, to share each other's experience, to communicate with each other. We are never completely successful in this. Our human condition is a bounded condition, bounded by death, bounded in death. There is a loneliness at the heart of each of us which we cannot overcome. Even the most perfect attempt at human sharing leaves us unsatisfied, leaves us alone. The fascination and the bitterness of sex consists in this fact. Sexual experience points to a total sharing which it cannot achieve.

However limited the success of our attempts to get to know another person, we have to continue to make the attempt, not only for his sake but for our own. It is only through our imperfect communication, our imperfect sharing, that we come to discover, not only the other, but also ourselves. Our stature as individuals is measured by the success of our attempt to share ourselves with other people.

If, however, all attempts to 'get inside' each other are thus largely unsuccessful, our attempt to 'get inside' the mind of Jesus is even further doomed from the start because his situation is, by christian definition, unique. However, it is clear from the new testament that the apostles were conscious of the fact that Jesus was conscious of the fact that he was related to the mystery, to his 'Father', in a special way. During his public ministry, Jesus communicated with his friends in the ordinary way: he talked with them, walked with them, laughed with them, ate with them.

Notice, however, how little, how surprisingly little, he seems to talk directly about God. He talks, almost exclusively, about people. In particular, he talks about that renewal of the human condition, of human community which, using biblical categories, he describes as the rule or kingdom of God. Moreover, he makes it clear that, through that mutual exposure which is his communication with his friends, he is leading them on to a critical decision in regard to their relationship to reality, to the ground of reality, to God.

The apostles, before Easter, never really see the point. They come to trust him, they come to lean on him ('Master, to whom shall we go?'), but they never really see that God is only discovered, revealed, in human relationships. They are always expecting him, since he seems to know God, to draw aside a veil, to show them himself and God (that *et* of *verus Deus et verus homo* again); and this he cannot do.

> Philip said, 'Lord, let us see the Father and we shall be satisfied.' 'Have I been with you all this time, Philip', said Jesus to him, 'and you still do not know me? To have seen me is to have seen the Father, so how can you say, "Let us see the Father"? Do you not believe that I am in the Father and the Father in me?' (Jn 14.8–10.)

Now, before we empty that conversation of meaning by setting up the reassuring categories of classical trinitarian theology, we must ask ourselves: is not Jesus pointing to a common factor in all our human discourse about God, a factor which I hinted at earlier by saying that *I* can only believe in the God I discover, not in somebody else's? In a recent paper, Sebastian Moore put it like this:

> The only thing you can give to your brother that is

> not going to alienate him from God and from himself
> is an honest and candid heart. The evidence for God
> from someone else is not what he says about God but
> what, believing in God, he uniquely *is*. The only
> religious authenticity today is the human authenticity
> of the believer.

Dom Sebastian says that the only religious authenticity
today is the human authenticity of the believer. In the
light of the quotation from St John's gospel, however,
I feel bound to ask: has it not always been the case,
however little we may have appreciated it, that the only
christian authenticity (I have switched the adjective because, to the christian believer, christianity is not simply
classifiable as 'a religion') is the human authenticity of
the believer? Jesus, of course, was not a believer—he
knew; however, the only qualification I should want to
make to Dom Sebastian's statement, in offering it as a
'translation' of what Jesus said to Philip, would be to
make it read: 'the evidence for the Father from Jesus is
not what he says about the Father but what, knowing the
Father, he uniquely is'.

In other words, if the last supper discourses were the
end of the story, the barriers to human communication
set up by the loneliness of our death-directed isolation
would not have been overcome. If the last supper discourses were the end of the story, Jesus would have been
no more capable of sharing himself with his friends than
any of us are. Thus far and no further. Poor Philip—
poor us. The apostles would have been left with the tan-
talising, frustrating glimpse of the mystery of the kingdom which drew that cry from Philip. The final state-

ment of the apostles about Jesus would have been: he knew—but we didn't.

Our human sharing is limited in the flesh, in the flesh of our death, in our death-bound condition. This is the heart of the matter, and if Jesus had it in him to take the business of sharing, of communication, any further, he had to deal with death, he had to do it in death. And he did. The explosion at the centre of christian history consists of the fact that the effect of his death was that these men knew.

On Friday, he died. On Saturday, all hope of their living must have been practically extinguished. The one man, their teacher, their friend, who had seemed capable, more than any man, of quickening their flesh, of enlightening their understanding, of sharing himself with them, had retreated into total isolation, into the total incommunication of death. In his death, their hope died; in his silence, 'they stopped speaking.

That was Saturday. On Sunday, they knew. On Sunday, they knew themselves in reawakened brotherhood, they shared with each other, across the barrier of death, which still stood for them, the first glimpse of a sharing that knew no barriers. They knew each other in the common consciousness of a human renewal that transcended their own limited ability to articulate it. In knowing themselves and each other reborn in brotherhood, they knew God. But what was the pattern of their discovery, the shape of the brotherhood? They knew him in the breaking of bread.[20] His death and their

[20] The identity between 'new knowledge in the risen Christ' and the birth to new brotherhood is even clearer in the case of Paul's awakening to christian (Easter) faith: 'Saul, Saul, why are

2+

ecstatic renewal, his silence and their birth to speech, were not unrelated, they were identical. The language of their brotherhood, the bread they broke, was his flesh broken for them. How were they to articulate, to locate, to polarise, this shattering newness? He helped them. He showed himself to them, the scars shining, in the context of their gathering, the context of their brotherhood (notice how important it is that almost all the resurrection appearances are in the context of a fraternal meal).

They unbolt the doors, rush out of the room into the street (in order to understand the paschal event in its unity, we have to do a little telescoping of the Lukan chronology). They have learnt to live. They have learnt that his death is their rebirth in the Spirit of God. They have learnt about being human, about brotherhood, the brotherhood of the new Adam, the brotherhood of the kingdom. They rush out of the room into the street. They have learnt to share, and they want to share their sharing. There is a power and an urgency in their proclamation that breaks the language-barrier. But all this that they are, all that they want to say, is him. He is the language of their brotherhood in the Spirit of God. How are they going to speak this new language; how are they going to talk Christ? In the sermons in Acts, the earliest surviving formulations of the attempt to talk new, they

---

you persecuting me?' (Acts 9.4). Not the least of the disadvantages that result from our tendency to regard infant baptism as the norm (whereas, in fact, it is a defensible exception) is that the identification of the birth into brotherhood with 'seeing the point' ('illumination', the title which the eastern churches have kept for the rite of christian initiation) is seriously obscured (cf *La Maison-Dieu* LXXXIX, 1967; *Concilium* IV, 3, 1967, 4–12).

still call him the servant of God. They had accepted for some time that he was the man sent by God, the messiah, the anointed servant. It will take some further time before they can find better words to describe a relationship which is incapable of adequate description. Gradually, tools are forged, and titles such as 'the Son of God', 'the word made flesh', 'the only-begotten of the Father', are employed. Some of these are new titles, some of them are old testament messianic titles whose meaning is radically transformed in the light of the Easter experience.

The apostles first encountered Jesus as a stranger, the teacher of Nazareth. They came, through deepening friendship, to know him and trust him, to 'believe in him'. But their personal adherence to Jesus was only transformed into christian faith when, by the power of the Spirit, they came, after Easter, to confess their faith in 'the God and Father of our Lord Jesus Christ'. This christian faith, their Easter faith in the divinity of Jesus, was born and articulated in the context of their awakening as a community reborn in the Spirit to conscious brotherhood in the love of God; a brotherhood, a sharing, articulated and structured by the bread shared, the body given. Christian belief is the belief of a community, conscious of their human communion in Christ, and living in the certainty that the brotherhood sown in the sign of the supper will eventually embrace all men. Christian belief is born in the context of brotherhood.

Christian belief is articulated in the context of brotherhood. By following the growth of the apostles' faith, we have already come to see something of what is entailed in this statement which follows on the one discussed in

the last few pages. Any discussion of the genesis of christian belief leads necessarily into a discussion of that act
by which this belief becomes articulate: that act which
is the central statement and expression of christian faith,
the eucharistic assembly. And so we have arrived at last,
although it has taken us some time to get there, at the
one indispensable basis for any balanced discussion concerning the nature, function, and method of christian
theology—the celebration of the eucharist.[21] Here, in
that commitment to brotherhood which is the new covenant between God and his people, we find the resolution
of the apparent dilemma whether christian theology is
about God or about man. Here in that fraternal meal
which is the expression of our personal faith, we find the
resolution of the apparent dilemma whether christian
theology is an individual or a collective project.

The celebration of the eucharist is the sacrament of
the church: the effective sign and central statement of
where the church comes from—Calvary; of where it is
—the brotherhood of believers; of where it is going to
—the kingdom of God. The church is in the world as
the sacrament or statement in sign of world history: of
where the world comes from—the loving hands of its
creator; of where it is—the ambiguous twilight in which

[21] 'If all Christian revelation is concentrated symbolically in the
liturgy, we are correct in saying that the liturgy is in turn recapitulated in the Eucharist. If the Lord himself is present in the
Eucharist, obviously this sacrament can be said to "contain the
whole revelation" ' (Moran, 126). The rest of this book is concerned with drawing out just a few of the implications of this
ancient christian truth which, if it were taken seriously, would
currently engage bishops, priests, and people rather more whole-
heartedly in the work of liturgical reform.

emerging brotherhood struggles for realisation with the
negative forces of denial, slavery, isolation, death; of
where it is going to—the consummated brotherhood of
all men in the daylight of the kingdom. (See further
chapter 5, pp. 138–67 below.)

In the celebration of the eucharist, we become articulate to each other, in God, not simply in the gesture of
our sharing, our eating and drinking, but also in the
words of the great eucharistic prayer, in which is specified and declared the meaning of our brotherhood in
relation to God's mighty works for man, in particular the
death and resurrection of his Son. (See further chapter
3, pp. 64–107 below.) It is to be noticed that this prayer
is made by one man, but that it is made as the expression of the community's belief. In this way (although
it is impossible here to go into any detail on the point)
the function of the ordained ministry in the church is
correctly stated. The man who makes the prayer does so
in virtue of the fact that he is our link-man with the
bishop, whom he represents, with the other christian
churches whose bishops are in communion with our
own, and with the whole series of churches whose
bishops have handed on what they also have received
from the apostles, and so from Christ. The authenticity
of our president's ministry is a principal element in
grounding the certainty that the eucharist we celebrate
is not simply the activity of an isolated sect but is, in
very truth, a communion in the body of Christ. But he
is not there to impose upon us the articulation of a belief which is not truly ours. He is there to express our
faith, the faith of the church. For this to be possible, of
course, we must each of us have received the word

through the church, the brotherhood, in the first place. But, as a general principle, it must be stressed that if the faith made articulate in the eucharistic prayer is to be truly our faith, the faith of the church, then not only must we have listened to the church (and, within the church, to the liturgical president whose foremost function is the proclamation of the gospel), but the liturgical president must have listened to us (how else would he know what we in fact believed?).

In the actual celebration of the eucharist, of course, this mutual sharing in truth, this mutual discovery of truth, is reasonably presupposed as the context of our celebration. This sharing is taken for granted in the celebration of the eucharist as the president makes the prayer, in a fixed form, and we assent to it. But this sharing in truth can only be safely taken for granted in the celebration of the eucharist if, in actual fact, it is taking place outside it. There is much work to be done in clarifying the relationship between the faith of the church, made articulate in theology, and that declaration of common belief which we call the exercise of the church's teaching authority, but the model for the work that we have to do must, I suggest, be the relationships that obtain in the celebration of the eucharist.

The church has the constant task of reformulating its simple, unchanging Easter faith, to enable it to articulate that faith, to witness to its belief, in changing situations.[22] To affirm that this task is the responsibility of

[22] To say this is not to say that any later reformulated affirmation of unchanging faith can ever deny, or call in question, an earlier solemn affirmation of that faith made in different circumstances and, therefore, in different language. I have tried to

the whole church, the whole eucharistic brotherhood, is not to deny the Christ-given duty of the bearers of apostolic office to declare that faith in the name of the church, once the *consensus fidelium* has been reached. There is no question of anybody, bishops or people, being entitled to 'impose their own opinions' on anybody else. The whole church has the duty of listening obediently to the word of God, and of declaring what they have heard to be the word of God. In the case of a declaration which the whole church wishes to be a declaration of the whole church (and not simply a statement of theological opinion), then the responsibility for making this declaration falls to those who hold apostolic office. The ultimate guarantee that the faith of the church, for which they must listen, and the declaration which they make, is not a betrayal of the word of God, rests not on the ingenuity of theologians, or the votes of an assembly, or on authoritarian power, but on the promise of Christ that he will, in the gift of his Spirit, be with his church all days until the consummation of the kingdom.[23]

---

discuss this question elsewhere: cf 'Dogmas and Doctrinal Progress', in *Until He Comes* (Dayton 1968) pp. 3–33.

[23] The church is an institution not because her official structures are often (regrettably) bureaucratic, or because ecclesiastical authority is often (regrettably) exercised according to the manner of secular power, or because she is a monarchy or a democracy (she is neither), but because that pattern of human relationships which constitutes the church is intelligible and, in its essentials, stable. Because most large-scale groupings of human beings articulate their pattern of relationships in the language of law (defining the rights, duties, and competence of the constituent persons), the church is always tempted to try to define,

Before ending this section, I should point out that, by thus setting the discussion in the context of the euchar-ist, a point of fundamental importance has emerged: namely, that all good theology is worship. Too often this is not the case; too often we have forgotten that 'ortho-doxy' and 'doxology' have a common root. Good theo-logy, the articulation of belief, is the adoring response of the christian mind to the saving word God speaks to his people.

Christian belief is expressed in the construction of brotherhood according to that belief. By using the cele-bration of the eucharist as a model, I have tried to in-dicate what I had in mind when I said that christian belief is born and articulated in the context of brother-hood. Now we must move on to see how that belief is expressed.

The christian is concerned, as is every man, with un-derstanding the situation in which he finds himself—his family situation, economic situation, political situation —and with responding appropriately to it. What sort of response is appropriate to him, specifically as a chris-tian? At this point one of the inadequate answers to the question with which I began: Is christianity about God or about man?, could reappear in a slightly different

achieve, and safeguard her stability through legal enactment. But constitutional law (although necessary) cannot be, for any society, the ultimate guarantee of the health and freedom of that society. This is a fortiori true of the unique society of the church, which is totally subject to the free activity of the Spirit. To attempt to safeguard the deposit of faith, or build up the body of Christ, by legal enactment, is a betrayal of trust in the truth-giving Spirit. Canon law is no substitute for corporate faith and charity.

form. It could appear in the form: the appropriate response of the christian to society consists in constructing
specifically christian structures: christian political
parties, christian plans for aiding developing countries,
christian hospitals, christian football teams, and so on,
and in doing all this alongside the 'normal' responses,
the 'merely human' responses expected of him as a
citizen of this world: paying taxes, working for Oxfam,
healing anybody, playing football with anybody, and so
on. But such an answer involves the classic misuse of
that little word 'and' in the proposition: christianity is
about both God and man; *verus Deus et verus homo*.
We have seen, however, that christianity is not about
God plus man; it is about God and man in the sense
that it is about being human in a new way, not about
being human in two ways at once.

Inevitably, in a short essay, I am oversimplifying
issues that are not simple. It would be dangerous non-
sense to limit the formally christian structures of the
church to the celebration of the eucharist (not only dangerous but impossible); I have been using the eucharist
as a model because it is the focus round which other
structures and activities operate, and from which they
draw their authenticity and meaning. In the present
context, it would be rash to assume that there is never
any place for christian political groupings, for christian
economic aid, for christian medical organisations, and
so on. The point that I am concerned to make is that,
in principle, our christian response to society is expressed in solidarity with other men in the secular
groupings, political, economic, cultural, in which we
find ourselves. It is here that the struggle for emerging

2*

brotherhood takes place. Specifically christian structures, except for those which are necessary to maintain
and deepen the world-wide communion of eucharistic
fraternity, are a kind of first-aid, an immediate response
to current needs when and where we see that the secular
structures cannot yet cope. But we have to work to make
them able to cope.

What has all this got to do with theology? The short
answer is: everything. To show how, and why, I must
first outline, rather schematically, some aspects of the
recent history of theological method. Some years ago,
theology was neatly categorised into fundamental theology (a rather ambiguous title, as Karl Rahner has
shown), positive theology (searching the scriptures and
the 'monuments' of christian tradition to find 'proofs' of
doctrinal assertions), and speculative theology (the formulation of conceptual syntheses to interpret the data
presented by the positive theologian). Positive and speculative theology were, in turn, divided into dogmatic
theology (concerned with the 'truths' of revelation) and
moral theology (how the christian ought to behave). The
most striking thing about this whole complex was its
abstraction, not in the positive sense of an interpretative
analysis in depth, but in the negative sense that it constituted a world on its own, only related with considerable difficulty to the world in which we live. This was
even true of moral theology for, although it professed to
handle concrete situations, it was less concerned to do
so than to provide an intricate network of a-priori principles on the basis of which the christian was supposed
to decide how to act in a given situation. There was a
paralysing divorce between the actual facts of life that

pressed upon us, demanded a response from us as christians, and the christian 'thing' which we felt bound to impose upon these facts. The facts themselves, political, cultural, economic, literary, were not regarded as a proper basis for strictly theological reflection. Moreover, the articulation of the christian assertion (it would be dishonest to call it a response) was so sophisticated that only an expert could be expected to handle it, with the result that theology became an exclusively clerical pastime, because only the clergy had been educated in the manipulation of the complex conceptual machinery.[24]

One of the early effects of that increasingly concrete or 'existential' approach which was sparked off by philosophical developments, and by the biblical and liturgical movements, was the proliferation of 'theologies of' this, that, or the other, which were, methodologically, an uneasy compromise between the old a-prioristic imposition of a theory, and the new tendency to articulate a christian response to the facts. So, just after the second world war, we begin to have a theology of work, a theology of play, a theology of railways, a theology of sleep, and so on. In the last few years, this tendency has been carried to the point that much that is labelled 'theology' seems to have little to do with christian revelation at all.

It would be improper for me to attempt to be dog-

[24] This is not to say that most priests became theologians. On the contrary, it was as difficult for the priest as for anybody else to relate 'theology', as he understood it, to concrete living. He therefore came to regard it as something immutable, which did not relate to concrete reality in any meaningful sense. It is this, rather than laziness, which explains why so many already overburdened priests 'never opened a book' after leaving the seminary.

matic about future developments in theological method, precisely because most of the work still remains to be done. On the basis of what I have said already, however, I should like to suggest a model which may help us to discover the place of theology in our own lives, and which may indicate the sort of thing that this theology might be. Not surprisingly, my model will once again be the celebration of the eucharist.

We are men, citizens of this world. That is a good starting-point. As such, we have the obligation of responding to our situation in the home, in the city, in all the affairs of human society. We are called upon to understand the situation in which we find ourselves, and to attempt not only to understand it, but intelligently to perceive and to become involved in concrete measures for its improvement. The degree to which our response is formally articulated will depend upon our education. We may be expert plumbers, poets, policemen, or politicians. We may be experts at nothing in particular, but we are still human beings.

As christians, we share with each other not only our general human situation (which sharing may seem to amount to little in practice, so far are we from realising the brotherhood of the kingdom), but we also share our specific situation as members of the eucharistic brotherhood, the sign in the world of the eschatological brotherhood of all men in the kingdom of their Father. We believe that our eucharistic situation, as hearers of the word, interprets for us the wider history of mankind, since Christ died for all men, and all history is the history of salvation.[25] We are not only men who are gath-

[25] To say this is not necessarily to indulge in unrestricted

ered by God round the table of the last supper (and therefore men for whom the celebration of the eucharist must become the authentic expression of our attitudes and concerns 'outside' it); we are also men who go out from the table of the last supper, having renewed our existential appreciation of what it means to be newly human in the Spirit of the risen Christ (and therefore men whose attitudes and concerns 'outside' the eucharist must become the authentic realisation of their sacramental statement in the celebration itself).[26]

When I say, therefore, that christian belief is expressed in the construction of brotherhood according to that belief, I am also saying that christian theology is the way men think who gather round, and go out from, the table of the last supper. And the way men think determines the way in which they act.

Against this background, the task of theology can be divided into two broad areas. On the one hand, all our thinking, talking, writing, will be 'theological' in a profoundly important sense, however 'secular' its form. If our christian faith in the God and Father of our Lord Jesus Christ is born and articulated in the context of

eschatological optimism; it is simply to say that nothing in human history lies outside the salvific activity of God. 'Everything in the history of the world is pregnant with eternity and eternal life or with eternal ruin' (Karl Rahner, 'History of the World and Salvation-History', in *Theological Investigations* v, London 1966, 99).

[26] 'The community we create liturgically is pointless unless it is continually reaching beyond itself, extending to bring in all creation. The liturgy, then, is a political force—a force constantly working to transform human society into its own, communal image' (Adrian Cunningham and Terry Eagleton, 'Community', in *Catholics and the Left* London 1966, 13).

human relationships, if the human fact becomes the grammar of our discourses about God, then, strictly speaking, there are no such things as 'non-theological factors' in christian existence. What makes a christian's politics, or poetry, theological, is not the use of religious terms and concepts, but the fact that his thinking springs from and expresses that vision of renewed humanity which he has received in faith and which he celebrates sacramentally. From this point of view, 'theology' is not a distinct discipline, but an interpretative framework within which our secular activity is carried out (would it be ridiculous to suggest that an instinctive realisation that this is the case explains and justifies the search for a 'catholic atmosphere' in a catholic school, however seldom that goal may have been achieved, or however bizarre the forms it may sometimes have taken?). There is, perhaps, an affinity between this use of the term *theological* and the similarly comprehensive use of the term *political* employed by writers of the New Left.[27]

On the other hand, even if one allows and encourages the global use of terms such as 'political' and 'theological', it remains true that both political theory and theology must also exist as independent disciplines in their own right. Formal theology, as an academic discipline, is something of which we need more, not less, at the moment. This is true not only of exegesis and biblical theology (whose task it is to present an ordered and thematic presentation of the word of God as originally

[27] 'Politics is not only discussion of certain aspects of human behaviour—it is a discussion of the structures and institutions which make a man what he is, for a man only comes into being through his society' (Cunningham and Eagleton, 'Politics', in *Catholics and the Left* London 1966, 4).

heard, retaining the language and imagery of the scriptures), but even more of systematic theology, or dogmatics, whose task it is to reinterpret the scriptural word in relation to the actual situation in which we find ourselves.[28] This latter task, of course, is not simply one of translating propositions, but of interpreting history. History is not simply succession, but change, and the theological task is to assist and interpret contemporary change in the light of that most radical change ever wrought in the human condition, the death and glorification of Jesus Christ.

Although not every christian is called upon to be a 'professional' theologian, it is nevertheless true that, if his general thinking and activity is to be 'theological' in the wider sense, then in the measure in which his circumstances and education allow, he must be engaged in the work of formal theology, in at least the same way that he is engaged (be it only through reading the *Guardian*) in contemporary scientific, political, or economic thinking.[29]

[28] 'I am vigorously opposed to any attempts to reduce the scientific character of theology and the austere rigour of its thought by shallow appeals to make it more vital, more apostolic' (Charles Davis, 'Theology and its present task', in *Theology and the University* London 1964, 121; cf his important essay, 'The Danger of Irrelevance', in *The Study of Theology* London 1962, 13–26).

[29] There is a real danger that in this country, 'implementing the decrees of the Vatican Council' will continue to be understood to refer to 'practical' changes, whereas in fact this implementation consists fundamentally in that change of theological attitudes which alone can make 'practical' changes intelligible and coherent. 'The so-called pastoral character of this council is nothing but a new dogmatic sensitivity. It would be a fundamental misconception, therefore, to consider this church assembly

This is an urgent need if, in the wider task of his general response to his situation, the christian is not to be fundamentally irresponsible and, indeed, if he is not to betray the word which he has, by baptismal faith, committed himself to hold. If his detailed, day-to-day response to his situation is not consciously sustained and influenced by the word he has received, the word made flesh which he shares in the eucharist, then one half of his life permanently denies and renders unintelligible (and therefore 'scandalous') the other.[30] I referred earlier in this chapter to the facile and dangerous identification of 'orthodoxy' with the mere repetition of suitable propositions. It is the truth, the living truth which, according to St John, will set us free, not simply a theory about truth. Christian witness is rendered far more sterile by

---

less doctrinal than the earlier ones, just because of its pastoral character. Some of those who hold minority views will be making a sad mistake if they accept the final decisions of the Council "because it is, after all, only pastoral", as if everything were to remain unchanged as far as doctrinal presentation is concerned' (E. Schillebeeckx *Vatican II: The Real Achievement* London 1967, 15).

[30] Thus that anti-intellectualism to which I referred at the beginning of this chapter results in an almost total failure to perceive, and so to respond to, practical pastoral needs. 'For the flight from understanding blocks the insights that concrete situations demand. There follow unintelligent policies and inept courses of action. The situation deteriorates to demand still further insights and, as they are blocked, policies become more unintelligent and action more inept. What is worse, the deteriorating situation seems to provide the uncritical, biased mind with factual evidence in which the bias is claimed to be verified. So in ever increasing measure intelligence comes to be regarded as irrelevant to practical living. Human activity settles down to a decadent routine, and initiative becomes the privilege of violence' (Bernard Lonergan *Insight* London 1958, xiv).

the failure of the gospel to activate, in all members of the church, a coherent, effective concern for human brotherhood, than by the fact that, in their attempt to articulate their faith, christians may sometimes 'say all the wrong things'. In the days of his flesh, the humanity (the 'body' in Hebrew usage) of Jesus Christ was the sacrament of the God we cannot see. His body, the church, is still the sacrament of the God we cannot see. It remains true that our evidence for God is not what we say about God but what, believing in God, sharing in God, we are. The only religious authenticity today is the human authenticity of the believing brotherhood, the body of Christ, the Son of God.

Finally, it should be pointed out that there is, with the awakening realisation that we are, as christians, primarily and immediately concerned with the construction of human brotherhood, a danger of underestimating the extent to which that kingdom for which we work, pray, and suffer, is not a kingdom of this world. It is not a kingdom of any other world either. It will be this world radically transformed in the love of God. The scriptural evidence, and all the facts of history, refuse to allow us to rest on the complacent assumption that the kingdom comes through 'everything continuing to get gradually better'. Indeed, if anything, the evidence points the other way: it suggests that the kingdom will finally come just when, through an accelerating process of human and cosmic deterioration, most of us have ceased to find it possible to hope at all. This is not completely surprising; it is just about the way things were on Good Friday afternoon. Perhaps the nearest we can get, therefore, to a 'peep into the future' is to suggest that, just as each of us, in the following of Christ, has to learn to 'let go', to die into brotherhood (and this is both a process and a terminal event), so also the 'coming of the kingdom' is not only a process, in which we are currently engaged, but will also be a terminal event, when the whole world 'let's go', when the whole world dies to live eternally in the Father's glory.[31]

We began by asking what christianity, and so theology, is about. Is it about God or about man? We saw that it is about both, but only in the sense that the human project becomes newly possible in the love of God released into human history through the death and glorification of Jesus Christ. We then saw that many of the false developments in theology can be traced to the unspoken assumption that, in understanding human nature, it is permissible to put up 'the individual' and 'the collectivity' as candidates struggling for power. History is, and will continue to be, pockmarked by this struggle, but the christian is committed to its rejection. For him, the growth of authentic brotherhood is the condition of possibility for, not the denial of, the free flourishing of the individual.

These preliminary questions led to the main thesis of this chapter: that christian belief is born and articulated in the context of brotherhood, and expressed in the construction of brotherhood according to that belief. If this thesis has any validity, in terms of theological method, then perhaps it has been shown why it is that the concreteness and relevance of any discussion of the eucharist or the other sacraments is determined by the

[31] Cf C. H. Dodd *The Apostolic Preaching and its Development* (London 1963) 95–6.

extent to which we have some rather clear ideas about the sort of thing that theology is, and its place in our wider human and christian commitment. That we have not been altogether on the wrong lines is suggested by the following quotation from the Vatican Council's *Constitution on the Church in the World of Today*:

> Though mankind today is struck with wonder at its own discoveries and its power, it often raises anxious questions about the current trend of the world, about the place and role of man in the universe, about the meaning of his individual and collective strivings, and about the ultimate destiny of reality and of humanity. Hence, giving witness and voice to the faith of the whole People of God gathered together by Christ, this sacred Synod proclaims man's high vocation, insists on a certain seed of divinity which he carries within him; for this reason it offers to mankind the Church's sincere cooperation in fostering that brotherhood of all men which answers to such a vocation (3).

2
The Eucharist: sacrifice or meal?

In view of the fact that the mass and other sacraments stand at the centre of christian living, it is surprising that it is extremely difficult today to draw up an outline theology of the mass which would be acceptable to all catholics. The reason for this is that two streams in contemporary theology meet head-on at this point.

On the one hand, it has been customary for manuals of theology to present the theology of the mass against the background of the definitions of Trent, with the emphasis on the notion of sacrifice. On the other hand, the biblical and liturgical revival, reaching its fullest expression in a descriptive theology of the sacraments, has emphasised the fact that 'the mass is a meal'.

If it is true that the biblical and liturgical insights urgently require a fresh explanatory, doctrinal synthesis, it is equally true that the definitions of Trent cannot, even implicitly, be regarded as a satisfactory starting-point for a eucharistic theology. Certainly this was not the intention of the fathers of Trent, who were concerned to combat certain specific errors; and because the council was careful to avoid making decisions in favour of one or other school of theology, its statements can only be understood against the background of the theological controversies of the period. We are still not free from the danger of a certain 'fundamentalism' in reading conciliar texts.

The Vatican Council's *Constitution on the Sacred Liturgy*, because of its magnificent synthesis of the language of Trent and the language of contemporary sacramental theology, should provide the basis for a renewed theology of the mass that can meet the demands of both the schools of thought mentioned above. This chapter is an attempt to provide the broad outlines for such a theology. In chapter 3 I shall concentrate on one element in the rite of mass, the *anaphora* or great eucharistic prayer, and try, in the light of certain well-tried principles of sacramental theology, to discover what conclusions can be drawn for our understanding of the eucharist from an exploration of the literary form of this, the most important of christian prayers. In chapter 4 I shall return, in more detail, to the problems of the relationship between the church's worship and the sacrifice of Christ. Finally, in chapter 5, I shall say something about the relationship between 'worship' and 'life' by drawing out some of the implications of our affirmation of the presence of Christ in the liturgical assembly.

The last supper
Any theology of the mass must regard as normative the scriptural accounts of the last supper. This is not to prejudice any questions concerning the relation between

the mass and Calvary, or the mass and the last supper; however such questions are answered, it is a matter of historical fact that the church, in celebrating its euchar-ist, has always been conscious of acting in obedience to the Lord's command—'Do this in commemoration of me'.

Moreover, the accounts of the last supper as we have them in the synoptics and in the first letter to the Corin-thians are influenced by the apostolic liturgy. We are seeing the last supper through the eyes of the early church as it celebrated the eucharist. Quite clearly, the primitive eucharist was a meal. The early church's un-derstanding of the meaning of that meal can be dis-covered from the terms used in the scriptural accounts.

(a) *Memorial and Covenant.* The primitive eucharist was a commemoration. Not a commemoration of the last supper, but a commemoration of Christ, and of Christ in his saving mysteries. The idea, incidentally, of a 'mere' commemoration (*nuda commemoratio*) would have been meaningless to the jewish mind. The func-tion, in the old testament, of a liturgical commemora-tion of the *mirabilia Dei* was at once to recall the mighty acts of God before his face, to remind him of his pledge of covenant-fidelity, and to recall them before the people, to arouse in them an authentic covenant-response. This was done in a 'eucharist' that was the expression of the gratitude and obedience of the celebrating people.

The old paschal meal was such a commemoration. It recalled the past act that sealed the covenant; it expressed, actualised, and deepened the covenant-rela-tionship in the present, and it was the pledge of covenant-fulfilment in the future. It drew both its significance and its efficacy from the initial sealing of the covenant in an historical act.

Our Lord, at the last supper, took the framework of this preparatory covenant-memorial (thus making his actions intelligible to the apostles), giving it an immensely richer and permanent significance by relating it to his coming *transitus*, which was to be the act sealing the new and eternal covenant (whether or not the last supper was actually the paschal meal, it was certainly understood by the evangelists to have a paschal significance). The last supper, and the new series of commemorative meals which, at his command, this supper inaugurated, also draw their full significance and efficacy from the act of covenant-union which they evoke. And it is clear, from the new testament evidence, that this new paschal meal is to carry, as had the old, a triple relationship to the past action which it evokes (the new *mirabilia Dei*: the death and glorification of Christ), to the present covenant-situation of God's people, born from the cross but actualised in the memorial, and to the future consummation of this new covenant-relationship (cf *Constitution on the Liturgy* 6, 10, 47). The clearest expression of this is St Paul's 'As often as you eat this bread and drink this cup you show forth the death of the Lord until he comes' (1 Cor 11.26). Within this general framework of a covenant-memorial-meal, the meaning of the rest of our Lord's words becomes clear.

(b) *He blessed*. In taking both the bread and cup, Jesus uttered a thanksgiving. This 'eucharist' (cf Mk 14.23

and parallels; 1 Cor 11.23) must again be seen in its old testament liturgical setting. The 'blessing of food' in the old testament, particularly on a solemn occasion such as the passover meal, was a blessing (praise) of God which, as specifying the meaning of the action which followed, blessed (hallowed) the food. This is the function of our Lord's prayer of blessing at the last supper, and so of the great eucharistic prayer in the christian liturgy. By this prayer the church makes explicit the action which is the 'memorial' of thanksgiving and intercession; it declares what it is doing. This pattern is in conformity with the received theory of 'matter and form' in sacramental theology. The 'matter' is a human action (never a 'thing'), the theological significance of which is specified, declared, achieved, by the accompanying word. It is this combination of rite and word which 'constructs' the efficacious sign of the presence of Christ in his mysteries. From the point of view of an integral liturgical and sacramental theology it is important to point out that the whole eucharistic prayer constitutes the 'form' of the sacrament, the consecratory prayer.[1]

(c) *Body and Blood.* Our Lord's words 'This is my body ... This is my blood' are certainly to be understood as stating a real presence of the Lord, but, since the mode of that presence is sacramental, the words are nevertheless to be understood in a symbolic sense. There has been a tendency in post-reformation theology to deny this in order to safeguard the doctrine of the real presence. Such a denial is unnecessary (apart from the

[1] Cf ch 3.

fact that some points of the defence have been rather weak: eg the emphasis on the verb 'is', which would have been absent from our Lord's aramaic) because the presence of the Lord in the eucharist is none the less real for being sacramental. The eucharistic action, the mass, is a sign, of which the consecrated species form an essential element.

The hebrew words probably used by our Lord for 'body' and 'blood' bring out, in their old testament usage, the full reality of what he is doing as an act of covenant-sacrifice.

> ... *basar* does not signify a principle or element of a living being, but rather the entire being in its concrete individuality, with emphasis on its external manifestation ... *basar* stresses the dynamic, creative power of life as manifested in the flesh. ... Thus, at the supper, Christ's use of the word 'body' signifies his entire self. He gives his disciples the concrete totality that is himself, therefore all the divine power of life of which his body is the external manifestation. In this sense his body is the sacrament of that divine δυναμις that is essentially opposed to sin and death and that is, therefore, essentially salvific.
>
> ... the constituting of brotherhood through a covenant was not only symbolized, but actually effected, through some rite of sharing blood. ... Jesus' use of the word 'blood' at the supper must be taken in a concrete sense as referring to himself in his totality as a living being, but with the emphasis on the living force 'within' him. At the same time, his act of sharing his blood means that he is sharing his soul, his

spirit, that he is establishing a brotherhood based upon a community of intention.[2]

There are two consequences of this. The first is that the words 'body' and 'blood' cannot be understood apart from the present participles attached to them. This is not 'simply' the Lord's body and blood. It is his 'given-for-you' body and 'shed-for-you' blood. This underlines the sacrificial nature of Christ's presence in the eucharist; Christ handed over both for us and to us. Christ is not present in the eucharist 'statically', but dynamically, in his *transitus*. This is why (but the point will be developed later) to share in this meal is to share in his pasch.[3]

The second consequence is that although the whole setting of this covenant-meal, and the use of these terms in particular, makes this meal a 'sign of covenant-sacrifice', the separate consecrations have no special significance (simply as separate) for 'showing his death'. There are two consecrations because there are two things to be consecrated; food and drink. But since both body and blood signify, to the Jewish mind, the whole reality of the person, there is no fundamental 'picture of bloody separation' in the distinct consecrations. The contrary theory has had a long and honourable history, but in origin it belongs to the same secondary (imposed) order of signification as does the commingling rite, in so far as this is understood to 'symbolise' the resurrection. The continued popularity of the theory is due to the

[2] Bernard Cooke sj 'Synoptic Presentation of the Eucharist as Covenant Sacrifice' in *Theological Studies* (1960) 25–6.

[3] Cf Cyprian Vaggagini *The Canon of the Mass and Liturgical Reform* (London 1967) 102–3.

fact that, for a long time, theologians were unable to see how a meal could be an adequate 'image' of Christ's sacrificial death.[4] And yet St Paul was always reminding us that the death of the Lord was shown forth by our eating of this bread and drinking of this cup. The principal conclusions to be drawn from this brief examination of the last supper must now wait until the notion of sacrifice has been explored.

Sacrifice

(a) *Sacrifice in general.* For many years now attempts have been made to outline the essential nature of sacrifice, as applicable to all religions, at all periods of their history. The story of these attempts is the story of a withdrawal in the face of a deeper understanding of comparative religion. It is the story of a-prioristic generalisations being discarded in the light of empirical evidence.

The first stage was to suggest that sacrifice consisted essentially in the destruction of the victim, in its immolation as a sign of its being made over to God. As a general theory of sacrifice this remains unacceptable even when the valuable distinction has been made between 'oblation' and 'immolation'; not least because there are plenty of forms of primitive sacrifice that involve no destruction of the materials used.

The second stage is to see the essence of sacrifice as

[4] St Thomas did not have this difficulty. His general principle is that '*celebratio hujus sacramenti* est imago repraesentativa passionis Christi' (*Summa Theologica* III, 83.1 ad 2, cf 75.1 and 79.1). His nuanced treatment of the secondary symbolism of the distinct consecrations is particularly interesting in the light of Fr Cooke's remarks quoted above (cf *ST* III, 76.2 ad 1).

giving something to God. This theory, which again fails to meet all the facts and is far too sophisticated for many primitive rites, still has a large influence in theology and popular piety. It colours many current explanations of the offertory rite in the mass and, indeed, underlies the generally accepted meaning of the word 'offer'. The theory is still frequently applied to the great eucharistic prayer in the mass, as if 'offering the sacrifice of Christ in the church' meant giving Christ (or the consecrated elements) to the Father (with the implied corollary that Christ is given back to us in the communion rite). The fact that nowhere in the liturgy of the mass is there any ritual action to express or support this theory has not been sufficiently adverted to. There are only four essential ritual elements in the eucharistic liturgy; they are the actions of Christ at the last supper. Food and drink are taken, they are made the centre of a prayer of thanksgiving ('blessed'), they are shared (the 'breaking of bread') and eaten. Two other ritual actions accompany the eucharistic prayer (setting aside the secondary gestures that have multiplied during the years, and which are probably to be removed by the present reforms): the elevation of the consecrated species for the adoration of the people, and the 'little elevation'. This latter gesture is to be understood as a 'presentation' of the sacrifice of Christ to the Father in the sense that it highlights, by a gesture, the 'recall' (memorial) nature of the eucharistic prayer; not in the sense that it denotes a giving of Christ, or the consecrated elements, to God.

The third stage, developed in a recent book of Fr Bouyer's,[5] is to suggest that the essence of any sacrifice

[5] English translation, *Rite and Man* (London 1963).

is a sacred meal. The way was paved for this insight by the increasing understanding of the importance of communion in the sacrifice, but Bouyer has taken the idea a stage further. And while it is true that, not for the first time, he is guilty of over-generalisation, his book is none the less important in that it brings out the fact that the essential meaning of sacrifice is that of a sharing (attempted or realised) of divine and human life, a communion, a union of heart and mind. This at once throws light on the covenant-structure of judaeo-christian sacrifice, for the purpose of the covenant is precisely to establish a sharing of life and interests between God and his people.[6]

On such a theory, then, the mass is not a sacrifice followed by a meal denoting communion in that sacrifice; it is a sacrificial meal (and here the theory joins forces with St Thomas, contemporary liturgical theology, and the exegesis of the last supper). The view that the mass is a sacrifice followed by a meal arose as a result of the general failure by the people (over many centuries) to communicate at mass. On the one hand, the impression was thereby given that only the priest offers the mass (in

[6] Cf Hans-Joachim Kraus *Worship in Israel* (Oxford 1966) 112-24. The following pages should make it clear that I am not 'attempting to prove that the Mass is a true and proper sacrifice by first elaborating a scientific definition of sacrifice-in-general, and then applying that definition to the eucharist' (Francis Clark *Eucharistic Sacrifice and the Reformation* London 1960, 258). Fr Clark is surely right in insisting that the sacrificiality of the eucharist is to be explained in its total dependance on the death of Christ. Nevertheless it is not unimportant to notice how it is that the action by which our Lord intended his sacrifice to be effectively commemorated is itself recognisable (descriptively, phenomenologically) as a 'suitable' expression of its sacrificial significance.

any sense). On the other hand, communion lost its sacrificial character and was considered as a purely receptive activity ('receiving holy communion'), distinct from the action of offering sacrifice.[7] The meal itself is the sacrifice, which is why the eating of the food by at least one person present is necessary for the integrity of the sacrifice (cf *Mediator Dei* cts 119, echoing Trent).

What, on this theory, becomes of the statement that the words of consecration constitute the essential moment of sacrifice? Simply this: by the eucharistic prayer (and, minimally, by the account of the institution) this human assembly becomes, actually and explicitly, God's holy people assembled in the act of christian sacrifice. These words formally express the connection between Christ's death and the action of this assembly. From this moment the action of the assembly is the effective representation of Christ's sacrifice; without this moment it cannot become so, even in the act of eating the meal (in the language of sacramental theology, without these words the 'matter', the meal, would not have been specified by the 'form'). The Council of Trent was concerned to safeguard the doctrine that the minimal rite that 'confected' or achieved the sacramental sign consisted of the central words of the 'form' and the performance by at least one person of the specified action. This was in opposition to the error that declared that, when the whole assembly failed to communicate (ie when the people did not communicate), there had not been a valid sacrament of the Lord's sacrifice. But Trent no more recommended this

[7] Cf Pierre-Yves Emery *Le sacrifice Eucharistique selon les Théologiens Reformés Français du XVIIe Siècle, Verbum Caro* (1959) 76–7.

seriously impoverished gesture (communion by priest alone) than it recommended that the entire eucharistic prayer be replaced by the account of institution alone.

(b) *The sacrifice of Christ*. It would be possible to object to the theory of sacrifice suggested above on the grounds that, if sacrifice necessarily involves a meal, how is the death of Christ a sacrifice?

In the first place, the death of Christ cannot be understood in isolation from his glorification. The data for theology here are not two separate, statically conceived events: a death and a return to life, but one event, the *transitus Christi*, the definitive pasch, with its distinct (but not separate) moments. For too long, ever since St Anselm, western theology was preoccupied with trying to understand the Lord's death as if death alone could redeem us. St Thomas's towering genius attempted the beginnings of a synthesis of western and eastern theology by his insistence that the death, resurrection, and ascension of Christ are all efficient causes of the redemption.[8] Today, one of the chief fruits of the biblical revival has been the recaptured realisation that the death of Christ alone would profit us nothing, that we must grasp Christ's redemptive act dynamically, as one sweep from cross to glory, as a process of liberation and glorification[9] (as St John insists throughout his gospel).

The second point is that the *transitus* of Christ is a unique event, and the fulfilment of all human religious activity. This may seem obvious, but it involves the realisation that, precisely as unique, the cross cannot be

[8] Cf *ST* III, 48.6 : 50.6 : 56.2 : 57.6.
[9] Cf *Constitution on the Liturgy* 6, 61, 81, 104, 106.

placed into a category of religious acts. Furthermore, any concept that denotes an authentic element in human worship should be applicable, with the necessary qualifications, to the death of Christ. This fact should warn the theologian to be careful to avoid introducing an imbalance into his treatment by exclusive concentration on any one of the many available concepts.

But although our Lord's life, death, and glorification is the fulfilment of all religious activity, the theology and history of the old testament provide a privileged set of concepts with which to attempt a description of the unique event. The basic concept in old testament theology is that of the covenant, and Christ himself is the fulfilment of the covenant-relationship. He is the new covenant, the union of the divine and human, the free acceptance by a man of the saving will of God. But although he is established as the new covenant by his incarnation (by the *gratia unionis*), he only achieves his full stature, he only becomes the 'Son of God in glory' by his definitive act of obedience, by his glorifying cross (cf Rom 1.4; Acts 2.36). The death and resurrection of Christ is the act by which the new and eternal covenant is sealed.

In the old testament the acts which inaugurated, expressed, and actualised the covenant-situation were acts of sacrifice. They were acts of sacrifice, not by some arbitrary connection but because the meaning of sacrifice is an attempted or achieved sharing of the divine life by man.

The answer to the objection, therefore, is that, apart from this one unique act which is the cross, all sacrifices are liturgical acts, symbolic rites in which man attempts formal expression of his relationship to God. Precisely because the human situation is one of total or partial separation from God, everyday human activity cannot 'show' a state of full union with God. This can only be expressed, as something not yet attained by ritual, symbolic activity. But the death of Christ, on account of its very perfection as an act of religion, demands no such ritual or liturgical expression. What links the 'sacramental' death of Christ and the sacrifices of primitive and old testament religion is not their formal structure but their significance: [10] the realisation of covenant-union. By virtue of this, Christ's death is indeed truly described as a sacrifice, as the perfect and final sacrifice.

(c) *The Church—a Community-in-sacrifice.* One of the most important doctrinal achievements of the Vatican Council's *Constitution* is its insistence on the central place of the paschal mystery in christian life and worship (cf note 9 above). The church is the new people of God, founded on the paschal mystery. She is adequately defined as a community participating in this mystery; she is the 'pleroma' of Christ and her every action is structured to the mystery in which she is grounded. Every act of the church, every act of each individual member of the community, is a paschal act: a sharing in the *transitus Christi.* This is above all true of those key acts which we call the sacraments, in the celebration of which the church concentrates, actualises, and shows forth her innermost nature.

But since one of the terms that can authentically de-

[10] Not the *sacramentum tantum* (which is the level of meal or rite), but the *res sacramenti.*

3+

scribe the paschal mystery is the term 'sacrifice', then the church is, by her very nature, a community-in-sacrifice, and every action of the church and of each of her members is a sacrificial act. As St Augustine put it 'Now a true sacrifice is every work done that we may cleave to God in holy fellowship'.[11] It is impossible to exaggerate the importance of this truth, of which the fathers were so conscious, and which post-reformation polemic has obscured due to the necessity of defending the sacrificial nature of one of the church's acts, the eucharistic assembly. The eucharist is unique as being the structural focus of the life of the community, as being that act from which all her other acts, sacramental and otherwise, draw their meaning and efficacy (cf *Constitution on the Liturgy* 10), but it is not as sacrificial that it is unique.[12]

Although the insistence that the whole life of the church, and of the christian, is a *sacrificium laudis*[13] finds a particularly clear expression in the reaction of the

[11] *Civitas Dei*. Cf the whole of this magnificent statement of the theology of sacrifice, quoted by Palmer *Sacraments and Worship* I, 280–3.

[12] In this context, the use of the word *oblatio* at the time of Trent is interesting: 'Since there is an *oblatio* in every sacrament, and since the eucharist contains the *oblatio perfectissima* of Christ at the supper...' (abp of Nicosia, in a speech to the council in October 1562. Cf *Conc. Trid. Freiburg* 1901ff XI, 61–2).

[13] 'Dans la mesure où le christianisme est une religion basée sur une intervention de Dieu, la démarche sacrificielle par excellence de cette religion ne pourra être que la réceptivité à cette action de Dieu, que l'émerveillement devant un tel geste: une action de grâces, une eucharistie... l'expression *sacrificium laudis* est équivalente de l'expression *eucharistia*' (Thierry Maertens, 'Pour Une Meilleure Intelligence de la Prière Eucharistique' in *Paroisse et Liturgie* XLII, 69).

apologists to pagan sacrifice, it is, of course, biblical in origin. Of particular interest is the unanimous patristic witness to the sacrificial nature of baptism. The unity of the 'sacraments of initiation' (baptism, confirmation, eucharist) in the baptismal eucharist kept the realisation of this truth alive in the early church. Today, a renewed theology of the paschal mystery, and a revival of interest in St Thomas's theology of the sacramental character as a *deputatio ad cultum*,[14] is helping to restore the balance.

The all-important point to be made is that, prescinding completely from the formal structure of the eucharist, prescinding completely from how the death of the Lord is shown forth in the eucharist, that eucharist is necessarily sacrificial because it is the act by which the paschal covenant-community expresses and achieves most fully its essential nature.

(d) *The sacrifice of the church*. All the sacraments, then, and above all baptism and the eucharist, the great paschal signs (cf *Constitution* 10), are sacrificial. Baptism is as truly a sacrifice as is the mass. But whereas baptism is the initiation of an individual into the community, the mass is the sacrifice of the whole community. At baptism, the death and resurrection of the Lord as being realised in this individual are shown forth by the sign of washing, of being plunged into the death-dealing, life-restoring waters (cf *Constitution* 6). At mass the death and resurrection of the Lord as being realised in this worshipping community is shown forth by the sign of the messianic covenant-meal.

[14] Cf *ST* III, 52.1 ad 2.

It might be objected that the other sacraments are not sacrificial in the way in which the eucharist is, because Christ himself (and so his sacrifice) is only 'really present' in the eucharist. But this is not the case. Christ is 'really present' in all the sacraments; it is only the form of that presence which varies.[15] In baptism, Christ is really present in the action of baptising. In the eucharist, Christ is really present in the sacrificial meal in several ways, one of which is his substantial presence as the food and drink for the sacrificial meal.[16]

Baptism is 'both sacrament and sacrifice' in the sense that these terms denote distinct concepts. Structurally, it is a sacrament of sacrifice; the sign and the signified sacrifice are not distinct realities or events. The mass is 'both sacrament and sacrifice' in the sense that these terms denote distinct concepts. Structurally, it is a sacrament of sacrifice; the sign and the signified sacrifice are not distinct realities or events.

It should be clear from the beginning of this article that there is no difficulty in establishing the *convenientia* of the meal as a sign of sacrifice. It is not any meal; it is the paschal covenant-meal and, as such, essentially sacrificial.

In view of its historical importance, there is one more problem that must be discussed, and that is the reconciliation of the sacrificial nature of the mass (or baptism, or prayer, or charity) with the unique and unrepeatable nature of Christ's perfect sacrifice on Calvary. One of the principal difficulties in any discussion of this most

[15] Cf ch. 5 and Fr Herbert McCabe, 'The Real Presence', in *The Clergy Review* (December 1964) especially 750.
[16] Cf *Constitution* 7. referred to below.

tangled question is that almost all the possible terms have been used, at one time or another, with meanings that are almost diametrically opposed. For example, the use of the term 're-presentation' (with the hyphen) is catholic in origin. But whereas I agree with Stephenson[17] in rejecting the term if it is intended to imply 'a making present again' of Calvary, I also agree with Thurian[18] that its use is permissible if the sense is that of memorial; the 'presenting again', the efficacious recalling to the Father of Calvary by Christ through the act of his body, the church.

Stephenson says of that hyphen:

> ... alas, the little hyphen does transform the theory; and awe and bad theology compensate ill for lack of understanding. Commemoration does not mean a re-calling, but a recalling, and the richness and pregnancy of this commemoration of Calvary in the Mass consists rather in the fact that the glorious 'Hero of Calvary', he who is forever the Crucified and Risen One, is there really present amidst the Chruch which his passion and resurrection called into being, and there dispenses to his bride, with hands that still bear the scars of their piercing, the fruits of his passion. Similarly with the little hyphen in re-present. Nowhere, I think, in St Thomas's discussion of the eucharist, nor generally in patristic literature, does 'repraesentare' bear this meaning in relation to the passion.[19]

[17] 'Two views of the Mass: Medieval linguistic ambiguities', in *Theological Studies* (1961) 588–609.

[18] *The Eucharistic Memorial, Part 2, The New Testament* (London) 76–100.

[19] 593. In regard to baptism, St Thomas uses the same word:

Fr Howell's translation of the council *constitution* seems faulty at this point. The *Constitution*, quoting Trent, has *repraesentatur* (6); Fr Howell translates 'again made present', which begs the question.

In catholic theology and popular piety we are still not entirely free from the danger of giving the impression that the mass in some sense 'repeats' Calvary, in some sense 'makes it happen again', in some sense 'adds' to the value of Calvary. As with so many theological problems, the clue to the resolution of this one consists in the fact that there is no special problem here at all. The mystery of the reality of the mass is the mystery of the 'pleroma', the mystery of the reality of created grace and our participation in Christ.

The praise and prayer of the church is true praise of the Father and a begging of his mercy without adding anything to the praise and prayer of Christ because it is a participation in his praise and prayer. Created grace is true friendship with God without adding anything to the uncreated grace who is the Spirit of God because it is a participation in the spirit.

The mass is truly a sacrifice without adding anything to the sacrifice of Christ because it is a participation in that sacrifice through faith and charity. Of course the reality (validity) of this participation is totally dependent on the initiative of Christ (cf any recent study of the meaning of *ex opere operato*).

Some of the false problems that have arisen here are the result of the deadening effect that a corrupt liturgy

---

'... passio Christi operatur quidem in baptismo aquae, per quandam figuralem repraesentationem' (*ST* III, 66.12.c).

has had on the consciousness, in the minds of the worshipping assembly, of the reality of Christ's (priestly) presence in them by grace. When the presence of Christ in the consecrated species is the only one which looms large in the consciousness of the faithful, then 'Christ now offering himself again' is thought of as referring, not to their self-offering in Christ, but to something happening 'out there', on the altar. In this connection, article 7 of the *Constitution* is of great importance: 'Christ is always present in his Church, especially in her liturgical actions. He is present in the sacrifice of the mass ... in the person of his minister ... under the eucharistic species ... in his word ... when the Church prays and sings.'

When priest and people, acting in co-operation with grace and in obedience to the Lord's command, reaffirm their obedience to God's covenant-will by celebrating that meal which, as memorial of Christ's death, carries this precise significance—then their prayer, their obedience, their action, are the prayer, obedience and action of Christ. It is misleading to say either that 'we offer Christ to the Father', or that 'Christ offers us to the Father'. The balanced statement is to the effect that, by the grace of Christ, our self-offering to the Father, expressed and sealed by our sharing in the meal, is a participation in his self-offering to his Father on Calvary.[20]

[20] 'Il n'y a pas deux sacrifices, celui de la croix et celui de l'eucharistie; il n'y a pas deux œuvres, celle du Christ et celle de l'Eglise; mais une seule œuvre et un seul sacrifice, accomplis par Christ, participés par l'Eglise' (Emery, 72).

The sacrifice of Christ is sacramentally represented in a human activity: a meal. As with every sacrament, the entire purpose of the visible rite is to embody, realise and express an inward worship;[21] an attitude of heart and mind and will: the visible rite has no independent, quasi-magical efficacy. As with every other sacramental encounter with Christ, the mass presents a challenge to faith and commitment. A person who has thus understood the relationship between rite and faith, between sacrament and sacrifice, and who is nevertheless not prepared to engage himself fully in the rite by communicating (though he may be prevented by circumstances) is not in a suitable frame of mind to offer mass at all, and his presence in the worshipping assembly is of doubtful value and significance.

On this whole question of the relationship of the mass to Calvary, it seems difficult to improve upon St Thomas's statements: '... sacrificium autem, quod quotidie in Ecclesia offertur, non est aliud a sacrificio quod ipse Christus obtulit, sed ejus commemoratio' (*ST* III, 22.3 ad 2); '... celebratio huius sacramenti est imago repraesentativa passionis Christi' (*ST* III, 83.1 ad 2); '... hoc sacramentum habet triplicem significationem; unum quidem respectu praeteriti, inquantum scilicet est commemorativum Dominicae passionis, quae fuit verum sacrificium ... et secundum hoc nominatur sacrificium' (*ST* III, 73.4).

The mass is a sacrifice in the sense that it is an effective memorial, recalling the 'true sacrifice' of Calvary, and achieving now, in the worshipping community, that

---

[21] A constant theme of *Mediator Dei*: cf CTS ed. 25, 27, 33, 98. Also, of course, the Vatican *Constitution passim*; especially 11.

covenant-union which is the purpose and meaning of the cross.[22]

Conclusion

The two attitudes mentioned at the beginning of this chapter are perfectly reconcilable once two points are agreed upon. The first is the fact that the mass is one of the seven sacraments. The second is that the relationship of meal to sacrifice within the structure of this sacrament is that of sign to signified.

The eucharistic sacrifice is that sacrament which, as effective memorial of Christ's saving death and resurrection, is the covenant-sacrifice-meal of the new people of God, recalling that covenant's sealing on Calvary, actualising the covenant-union in the worshipping assembly (in so far as they co-operate in faith and charity) and anticipating the covenant's perfect fulfilment in the eschatological messianic banquet.

In other words, the mass is that 'memoriale ... mortis et resurrectionis suae: sacramentum pietatis, signum unitatis, vinculum caritatis, convivium paschale, in quo Christus sumitur, mens impletur gratia et futurae gloriae nobis pignus datur'.[23]

[22] This is the perspective of Trent; cf the passage from the 22nd session 'in coena novissima ... applicaretur' (Denzinger 938).

[23] Vatican *Constitution* 47. In addition to the *Magnificat* antiphon for second vespers of the feast of *Corpus Christi* (the *O Sacrum Convivium*), the council is quoting a passage from Augustine (*In Ioannis Ev Tract* XXVI, cap vi, n 13—cf PL 35, 1613) which is used for the same purpose by Trent, Session XIII, ch. 8: cf Denzinger 882.

3*

3
The eucharistic prayer

At the beginning of the previous chapter, I suggested that there were two broadly distinct contemporary approaches to the theology of the eucharist. These two approaches to the problem are rooted, not simply in two different theories about the mass, but in two different views as to the correct method according to which a theology of the mass should be developed. If one's starting-point is the theological assertions of catholic theology over many centuries, then it will seem 'obvious' that the mass is a sacrifice, but not so obvious how it is. If one's starting-point is the fact of the liturgical assembly (the concrete sign), then it will seem 'obvious' that the mass is a meal, but not so obvious how the celebration of this meal is the offering of a sacrifice. The waters of the debate are muddied from time to time by reminders that the eucharist is not an ordinary meal (I am unaware that any serious scholar has ever said that it is), and that the severance of the eucharist from the 'ordinary' meal (the *agapē*) took place early in the church's history.

Jungmann[1] has summarised the process by which the increasingly stylised liturgical act came to be separated from the 'meal' properly so-called. But it is interesting to notice that the eucharist was still preceded by a meal on Maundy Thursday evening at the time of Augustine; a practice which hung on into the fourteenth century in some places. The only novelty, therefore, in the contemporary tendency to celebrate an 'ordinary' fraternal meal in connection with the eucharist is that it is now our custom, due to that instinctive reverence which led to the emergence of the eucharistic fast, to do so after the liturgical act, and not before it. But, whatever the history of the relationship of the liturgical act to the ordinary meal, it remains true that the eucharist, when it came to be celebrated independently, nevertheless consisted in the taking, blessing, sharing, and consumption of food and drink, an activity which, on any account, is some sort of a meal.

Methodologically, the two approaches to the problem are mutually irreconcilable, but this does not mean that to select one of them is necessarily to render oneself incapable of incorporating the insights acquired by the other. The previous chapter was an outline of a theology of the mass adopting the second approach which, so it seems to me, not only situates correctly the concepts of *sacrifice* and *sacrament*, but is positively demanded

---

[1] Cf *Missarum Sollemnia* (Paris 1956–1959) I, 40. Throughout this chapter, references are to this French edition, because the English edition (*The Mass of the Roman Rite* London 1961) is abridged and lacks the critical apparatus.

by the biblical, liturgical, and historical data. In this chapter I want to take the argument a stage further by concentrating on one element in the rite, the great eucharistic prayer or *anaphora*. The justification for doing so may be briefly stated as follows.

Any sacrament (including the mass) operates at three levels: the level of the 'mere sign' (the *sacramentum tantum*) or empirical reality; the level of the significance which christian faith attaches to that sign so far as the relationships of human beings *in Christo* are concerned (the 'ecclesial' level, or *res et sacramentum*); the level of the significance which christian faith attaches to that sign, and to that pattern of christian relationships, so far as the relationship of mankind to God is concerned (the level of grace, or *res tantum*). The sacrament is celebrated, the sign is enacted, in order that the church may enter more deeply into the spiritual reality indicated in the sign. So far as the eucharist is concerned, classical theology has always recognised that the *res tantum* of the celebration is the unity of the church:[2] the ingathering of God's scattered people by his redeeming grace, an ingathering 'foreshadowed from the beginning of the world', 'prepared for' in the dispensation of the old covenant, 'founded' in the cross of Christ, now 'made manifest' by the power of the Spirit in the pilgrim church—whose life and celebration herald its 'glorious consummation at the end of the ages'.[3] There

---

[2] 'Eucharistia est sacramentum ecclesiasticae unitatis' (Aquinas *Summa Theologica* III, 73.2); '. . . res hujus sacramenti est unitas corporis mystici' (73.3). Cf Thierry Maertens, 'Pour Une Meilleure Intelligence de la Prière Eucharistique', in *Paroisse et Liturgie* XLII, 50–1.

[3] These phrases describing the various stages in the 'growth' of

is little likelihood of disagreement about the meaning of the mass at this level.

Disagreements about the meaning of the mass at the level of the *sacramentum tantum*, the visible sign, can be presented at the bar of liturgical and historical research, because here we are dealing with empirical reality, and are not dependent upon the light of faith for our ability to discern whether one description of the mass at this level is more or less accurate than another; whether the rite as performed at one period in the church's history is more or less in conformity with the rite as celebrated by the apostolic church.[4]

The real difficulty arises at the intermediate level, that of the *res et sacramentum*. It is at this level that theological theories, concerned to interpret the significance of the rite, increase and multiply. How is it that the celebration of the rite achieves and expresses the unity of mankind in the grace of God? If the answer to this question is: through the participation by the church in the sacrificial death of Christ, then how are we to understand the rite as indicating this truth (and if it does not indicate it, we have no sacrament—sacraments cause by signifying)?

Of the four elements in the eucharistic rite, as we find them recorded in the new testament, and as they are found in all liturgies at all periods of the church's his-

---

the church are taken from the Vatican Council's *Constitution on the Church* 2.

[4] There is a qualification to be made here. The extent to which the rite may vary from its apostolic norm without betraying the will of Christ (eg may rice be used, or must it be bread?) is a question which can only be decided by the Spirit-guided community of believers.

tory, three (taking, sharing, eating) are gestures, and
one (the 'blessing': the *anaphora*) is a form of words.[5]
It is, in its entirety, the *forma sacramenti* (which, as in
the case of the other sacraments, does not mean that, in
cases of emergency, a truncated version of the prayer will
not suffice to make the gestures meaningful, and so to
'set up' the sacramental sign).[6] As the form of the sacrament, it is the *anaphora* which determines the meaning
of the gestures, the action (the *materia*) which it interprets.[7] It is therefore the case that, on the one hand, the
meaning of the mass can only be grasped through a study
of the eucharistic prayer and, on the other hand, that
the whole prayer must be studied: its literary form, pat-
terns, and rhythm, not simply isolated words and phrases
taken out of context.

The theology of the mass is, as is any theory, the interpretation of facts. The facts with which we are con-

[5] ' "Faire ceci" signifiait d'abord prendre, bénir, consacrer et
partager, mais aussi manger et boire, comme le demande ex-
plicitement la lettre aux Corinthiens' (Louis Ligier, 'De la Cène
de Jésus à l'Anaphore de l'Église', in *La Maison-Dieu* LXXXVII,
1966, 22). '. . . les quatre gestes de Jésus prenant le pain, rendant
grâces, rompant et distribuant, sont repris dans les quatre temps
de la messe, offertoire, canon, fraction et communion' (Ligier, 26.
Cf Max Thurian, *The Eucharistic Memorial. 2. The New Testament* London 1961, 35).

[6] Aidan Kavanagh ('Thoughts on the Roman Anaphora', in
Worship XXXIX, 9, 1965, 515–29, and XL, 1, 1966, 2–16) speaks of
'a gradual demise in regard for the whole anaphora as consecratory' (6).

[7] Cf Thurian, 36. '. . . la prière eucharistique est l'explication
de *l'action* exécutée pour répondre à l'ordre du Seigneur: *Faites
ceci* . . .' (H. Manders, 'Het eucharistisch gebed', *Tijdschrift voor
Liturgie*, 1967, 6–24; quoted from the summary in 'Table ronde
sur les projets de réforme du Canon', *Paroisse et Liturgie*, 1967,
no 3, 249).

cerned are a complex activity (the rite) that forms an image, picture, or sign. It is the thesis of this chapter that the dominant image to be interpreted by any sound theology of the mass must be the eucharistic rite itself as celebrated, in word and deed, in conformity with the mind of the apostolic church. Because the function of the *anaphora* is to articulate, to declare, the meaning of that dominant image, any sound theology of the mass must be centrally concerned with the significance attached to this prayer by the apostolic church. Later in its history, the church is at liberty to complicate the rite, at liberty to amplify its understanding through a more fully reflexive awareness of what it is doing in enacting this sign, but it may never depart from, declare itself at variance with, the eucharist as that existed at the period of the church's origin.[8]

In the next section, I shall be concerned to make some precisions concerning, and to answer some possible objections to, this method of approach. Then I shall summarise the findings of contemporary scholarship as to the nature and meaning of the great eucharistic prayer. Finally, I shall suggest that, during the course of the

[8] I shall refer later on to the problem of that reform of the canon of the mass which is so urgent a pastoral need in our own day. For the moment, I simply wish to stress that, in regarding the apostolic period as normative, I am not recommending a return, either theologically or liturgically, to some mythically 'pure' anaphora. I fully accept Fr Vagaggini's criticisms of such a procedure (cf *The Canon of the Mass and Liturgical Reform* London 1967, 140–4) and am in complete agreement with him when he says that 'any new anaphora has the right and the obligation not only to be deeply theological but also to reflect, in its own particular way, the theological interests of the Church of our day' (144).

church's history, the image of the rite itself[9] ceased to be the dominant image for theological reflection, and was supplanted by other, secondary images which, however valid and useful on their own, could only, when they came to supplant the basic image of the 'sign of the covenant-supper', exert a distorting influence on eucharistic theology and practice.

To begin with, it must be made absolutely clear that the problem with which we are faced is one of theological balance and intelligibility, not one of orthodoxy or heresy. It is not a problem of orthodoxy (at least in the restricted sense in which this word is usually understood) because, as a catholic, I do not believe that, however defective may have been its theory or practice at different periods in its history, the church has ever been allowed by Christ fundamentally to betray its mission by formally adopting a position which is radically incompatible with the truth which it serves. I do not share the attitude of those people who would brand as heretical any individual or school of theology with which they happen profoundly to disagree.

It is a problem of balance: but to say this is to say a great deal. The church may be protected by the Spirit

[9] By the 'rite' I do not mean the rubrics, or the regulations for celebrating the rite, but that ritual celebration as it exists in the concrete. In other words, the worshipping assembly is itself a constituent element in the sign or sacrament. This is not to deny the possibility (repeatedly asserted by the magisterium) of celebrating a seriously impoverished rite (mass without a congregation), but it is to register a protest against those theologies of the mass which would take the minimal, impoverished rite as the norm, and which, as a result, regard the presence and activity of the worshipping people as theologically unimportant (however much they may insist on its 'pastoral desirability').

from the formal denial of the deposit of faith, but a lively historical consciousness is making all of us more aware of the fact that the church is not prevented from the most extraordinary aberrations, in both theology and practice, arising out of undue concentration on one or other aspect of the truth, on account of the blindness engendered by hasty responses to historical pressures, or simply to a slow and unrecognised drift from concerns and attitudes that should be central to church life and witness. So, for example, it is perfectly orthodox to assert that the mass is the expression of christian fellowship in a fraternal meal, or that it is a truly propitiatory sacrifice, or that it is a memorial of the death of Christ, or that it is, on the part of the presiding minister, a priestly act, and so on. But if any one of these unexceptionable statements is too frequently asserted on its own, without the question being asked how this truth is realised in the concrete, or how this truth relates to other truths which must also be asserted (and which may, perhaps, be more fundamental than that which is currently being stressed), then it can happen that the resulting understanding of the mass, whether on the part of individuals or of the church as a whole, is so seriously distorted as to have disastrous consequences for the church's life and mission.[10] This tragic state of affairs can, it must be re-

[10] Illustration of this point is probably unnecessary, but it can hardly be denied, for example, that the reiterated and isolated assertion that the mass is, on the part of the presiding minister, a priestly act, leads to an under-emphasis of the more basic truth that it is a priestly act on the part of the whole people. The result is an understanding of the ministry which is something less than christian (cf ch 6), and it is hardly surprising that a reaction to this distortion should give rise to a complementary distortion that would find no specific intelligibility in the role of the minister.

peated, come about without there being any question of formal denial of any aspect of the total truth, and therefore without there being any question of orthodoxy, as that word is commonly understood.

The problem with which we are faced is one of intelligibility, because it is perfectly possible to make statements which, in the context of their origin, are unimpeachably orthodox, but which may yet be totally ineffective as a means of communicating truth to ordinary people. It may be true that 'at the consecration Christ comes down upon the altar and there renews his offering to the Father'. But what does it mean? How are we to understand the phrase 'comes down'; what does it mean for Christ to 'renew his offering'; what are we doing the while? If it is said that Christ 'takes our offering and makes it his own', what, once again, does this mean? How does it relate to what this group of people, assembled in this room, are doing, in the usually accepted sense of what it means for people to 'do' something?[11] It is clearly impossible, within the limits of this chapter, to attempt a detailed answer to these and many other equally interesting questions. All that is being offered is a framework within which it may be possible to give an intelligible account of our activity. To expect such an intelligible account to be possible is not to rationalise the mystery of our redemption. The human mind can never compass the mystery of God's redemp-

[11] At the risk of labouring the point, it must be insisted that I am not suggesting that phrases such as those quoted are meaningless; I am only making a plea that we never cease from asking what that meaning is (cf the preface to Sebastian Moore's brilliant book *God is a New Language* London 1967).

tive love, but it does not help to identify that mystery with a series of category mistakes.

One possible objection to the method to be employed in this essay would be that surely eucharistic theology has always been an interpretation of the meaning of the eucharistic prayer, and that it is therefore difficult to see wherein lies the novelty of this approach. However, while it is true that theology has used as its principal sources certain words and phrases drawn from the new testament accounts of the last supper, and contained in almost all *anaphoras* (the denomination of the food and drink as the body and blood of the Lord; the Lord's command to 'do these things in *anamnesis*'), it has nevertheless frequently failed to pay adequate attention to the context, the literary form, of the prayer in which these phrases occur, as that prayer-form was employed by the Lord himself or by the apostolic church.[12]

Another objection might be that, by going back to the jewish prayer-forms that underlie the new testament and apostolic 'eucharists' one is indulging in 'archeologism', and failing to show a proper confidence in the Spirit's guidance of theological and liturgical development down the ages. This objection cannot be answered adequately except in the light of a much wider discus-

[12] 'C'est un fait que les théologies courantes sur l'eucharistie, en général, ne font aucune place à "l'eucharistie" au sens premier du mot, à la grande prière eucharistique traditionelle' (L. Bouyer *Eucharistie: Théologie et Spiritualité de la Prière Eucharistique* Tournai 1966, 11). Fr Bouyer's massive study of the eucharistic prayer appeared shortly after I had written this and the following chapter. It was a matter of some satisfaction for me to discover that so considerable a scholar as Fr Bouyer has, from a painstaking analysis of the jewish and early christian texts, reached *theological* conclusions so close to my own.

sion of doctrinal development than is possible here. I shall merely repeat the assertion that a belief in the Spirit's guidance of the church through history does not entail a belief that the tradition[13] is necessarily free from a quite considerable distortion and impoverishment as the gospel is translated from one cultural milieu into another, and that it is entirely proper continually to search the sources of christianity to see whether important elements in the total christian consciousness may not, from time to time, have been obscured and forgotten, in order that, by the reintegration of such elements into our contemporary consciousness, we may arrive at a greater fidelity, in theory and in practice, to the word of God.

Is there not, however, a third and more fundamental objection that could be raised against the declared purpose of this essay: namely, that our knowledge of the origins of christian liturgy in the new testament period is still so imperfect, there are still so many serious and important questions that are unanswered, that anything said here can surely be no more than flimsy hypothesis (hypothesis, moreover, the selection of which probably depends less on scholarly objectivity than on immediate, short-term pastoral concern)? This objection has to be

[13] By the 'tradition' I do not mean simply the *monumenta*, but the whole complex of beliefs, attitudes, practices, that go to make up the concrete reality of the living church. So, as examples of such distortions, one could mention such things as that debilitating individualism (whether its causes are to be found 'inside' or 'outside' the church) from which the Spirit, over long periods, did not preserve his people; the failure of the church to see itself, in the concrete, as a community of witness to the risen Christ, and so on.

met in two stages. In the first place, this essay is not a piece of scholarly work in either exegesis, biblical theology, or liturgical history. It is a piece of popularising speculation. If the conclusions of contemporary exegetes, biblical theologians, and liturgical historians are seriously defective and erroneous, then the argument offered here is reduced in value if not, indeed, rendered positively harmful. Theology, like all scientific disciplines, is a collaborative affair, and this is the risk which the theologian takes. His only alternatives are either to say nothing at all, or resolutely to ignore the questions put to him by experts in other fields and by the demands of the concrete pastoral situation, and simply to repeat, as isolated and unhelpful assertions, whatever earlier theologians may have said on the subject. I prefer to take the risk.

In the second place, what are the areas of uncertainty to which the objection refers? Without attempting an exhaustive list, they certainly include such questions as the following: was the last supper a passover meal? was it some other jewish religious meal to which our Lord, or the apostolic church, attached paschal significance? what was at the forefront of the consciousness of the early church as it celebrated its eucharist? was it simply aware of table-fellowship with the risen Lord? was it continuing that series of meals it had shared with him in the forty days following Easter? was it consciously transposing the passover meal into its own situation and relating it to the death of the Lord? was it rather consciously repeating what had been done at the last supper? and so on.[14]

[14] Amongst the abundant literature currently available on the

Simply to list those questions and to admit, quite calmly, that to most if not all of them there is not complete unanimity in the replies of the experts, is to notice that this considerable uncertainty operates within a wider area of certainty, and that this wider certainty is quite sufficient for the purposes of this essay. The certainty to which I refer is that, when celebrating its eucharist, the church, through the voice of the presiding minister, utters a 'blessing', a 'eucharist', as the Lord himself had done the night before he suffered and that at least until such time as through the incorporation of considerable numbers of gentile converts the church went through the first of those 'cultural translations' which mark its history, in uttering this blessing it was employing a prayer-form which had been in use for centuries before our Lord's time, and which was still in use at the period in question.[15] In other words, if the general principle is admitted that the meaning of the eucharistic prayer must be of central significance for eucharistic theology, and if it is the case that we know the invariant structure which such a 'eucharist' had in the jewish religious culture in which the church was born, then we are in a position to say something of fundamental importance concerning the contribution which this central

---

exegesis of the new testament witness, a fine article by David Stanley sj should be noticed: 'Ecumenically Significant Aspects of New Testament Eucharistic Doctrine', in *Concilium* IV 3 (1967) 23–6.

[15] 'The very originality of the christian eucharistic prayer can hardly be grasped apart from its development out of the literary genre of Jewish prayers of blessing or benediction' (Kavanagh, 518, where he provides ample bibliographical witness to the increasing realisation of the importance of this point).

concept of 'eucharist' must make to any balanced under-standing of the mass.[16]

The title 'eucharist', 'the liturgical name which the "Lord's Supper" has finally been given preferably to any other, has been taken from that *eucharistēsas* (*-eulogēsas*) of the (New Testament) narratives'.[17] It is therefore clear, on the methodological principles stated above, that to understand what sort of thing a 'eucharist' is will be crucial for our understanding of the mass, for the meaning of *eucharist* is the meaning of the mass. A glance at the English versions of the new testament narratives of the last supper shows that our Lord's prayer of 'blessing' is variously described as a 'giving', 'offering', or 'returning' of thanks.[18] The history of eucharistic theology and practice might have been very different if

[16] There is increasing agreement amongst the scholars that, in our attempts better to understand, and so more adequately to reform the liturgy of the mass, 'tout ... converge vers le Canon' (Introduction to 'Le Canon de la Messe', in *La Maison-Dieu* LXXXVII, 1966, 3).

[17] J. P. Audet, 'Literary Forms and Contents of a Normal Eucharistia in the First Century', in *The Gospels Reconsidered* (Oxford 1960) 25. This essay first appeared in *Studia Evangelica: Papers Presented to the International Congress on 'The Four Gospels in 1957'*, eds K. Aland et al (Berlin 1959) 623–62; it has also appeared in French in *Revue Biblique* LXV (1958) 371–99.

[18] In the four accounts of the institution in the new testament, RSV always uses 'when he had given thanks' for *eucharistēsas*; NEB has 'offered thanks' (Mt 26.27; Mk 14.23), 'gave thanks' (Lk 22.19), 'after giving thanks' (Lk 22.17; 1 Cor 11.24); JB has 'when he had returned thanks' (Mt 26.27; Mk 14.23), 'when he had given thanks' (Lk 22.19), 'gave thanks' (Lk 22.17), 'thanked God' (1 Cor 11.24). *Eulogésas* (Mt 26.26; Mk 14.22) is rendered by 'blessed' (RSV), 'having said the blessing' (NEB), 'when he had said the blessing' (JB).

more attention had been consistently paid to these words, instead of which

> critical and theological reflection indeed do not appear to have devoted an effort (in this regard) proportional to that which was actually displayed, with so much insistence and complacency, around the three short sentences: 'This is my body', 'This is my blood', and 'Do this in remembrance of me'.[19]

Can we be satisfied that to describe the prayer of Jesus (and so the christian *anaphora*) as an act of 'thanksgiving' does full justice to that genre of jewish prayer which, taken over by the apostolic church and employed for its own purposes, is described as a 'eucharist'? The experts seem increasingly to be agreed that we cannot. It is difficult to overemphasise the influence on contemporary studies of the *anaphora* of the article by J. P. Audet which has just been quoted. In view of the critical analysis to which Audet's view has been subjected over the last ten years, and of the measure of acceptance which it has won, it would seem to be fully justifiable, in what follows, to take his conclusions for granted.[20]

In the first place, a 'eucharist' (or, rather, the jewish 'benediction' or *berakah* which underlies it) is essentially an act of worship. This point may seem too obvious to need making, but it can serve as a warning

[19] Audet, 25.

[20] Audet's findings are accepted, for example, by Betz ('Sacrifice et Action de Grâces', in *La Maison-Dieu* LXXXVII, 1966, 79); Denis-Boulet ('Notions Générales sur la Messe', in *L'Eglise en Prière* Tournai 1961, 260); Jeremias (*The Eucharistic Words of Jesus* London 1966, 109, 118); Kavanagh (the best recent treatment of the problem in English); Maertens (99); Thurian (38); and Vagaggini (20).

against the more extreme statements of 'secular religion-ists', who would make of the eucharist simply a fraternal gathering, with little explicit reference to the God whose saving acts are evoked, celebrated, in the assembly.

In the second place, a 'eucharist' is essentially a communal action, a prayer made in the presence of, and in the name of, an assembly of people, as the *Constitution on Liturgy* makes clear (eg 26, 27). It follows from this that the function of the individual deputed to 'make the eucharist' in the assembly cannot be defined in abstraction from that community in which, and for which, he exercises this function.[21]

In the third place, a 'eucharist' has a threefold structure and, if the celebration of the christian eucharist is truly to be the dominant image for subsequent theological reflection on the nature and meaning of the mass, it is of the greatest importance that this threefold structure is respected, so that the primary elements of the prayer remain the primary basis for reflection. Secondary elements there may be, and it is undoubtedly the case that liturgical practice and theological theory came to attach a disproportionate significance to them. To demand a return to the original proportions in the importance we attach to the primary and secondary elements

[21] Commenting on the significance of the phrase *famulo tuo* in the Roman canon, Maertens says that: 'Le prêtre chrétien ne se définit pas par lui-même, comme le prêtre paien: il est défini en référence à un peuple ou à une famille.... Cette conception du "service" est particulièrement importante dans l'Eucharistie, d'abord parce que, ainsi que nous venons de le voir, elle assure au sacerdoce chrétien sa nécessaire référence à la communauté, mais aussi parce que la notion du service est caractéristique du sacrifice même' (57). Cf *Paroisse et Liturgie*, 1967, no 3, 256–8.

respectively, so far as our theology is concerned, is not to demand that the secondary elements be overlooked, much less that the doctrine articulated in their theological development be denied.

The first element in this threefold structure of the classic *berakah* is

the 'benediction' proper, which gives its name to the literary genre as a whole ... always rather short, more or less stereotyped in its form, leaning towards the invitatory genre, an enthusiastic call to divine praise.[22]

The second element is the declaration of the motive for the assembly's praise. This motive is always declared to be a *mirabile Dei*, a wonderful work of God. Accordingly,

the psychological pattern underlying the spontaneous 'benediction' is above all that of admiration and joy, not of gratitude, which remains subordinated, in fact, to the fundamental feeling of admiration, and is therefore secondary.[23]

[22] Audet, 19. Cf Kavanagh, 519.

[23] Audet, 19. Insofar as the christian eucharist is concerned, it would perhaps be misleading to press too far the distinction between 'praise' and 'thanksgiving'. 'Praise' concentrates on the person praised, 'thanksgiving' on the gift received from the person. In the christian dispensation, the person and the gift so completely coincide as to become identical, and it is therefore hardly surprising that, as Fr Audet himself notes: 'the "benediction" proper was progressively bent towards "thanksgiving" ' (34). Provided that this thanksgiving is still understood as shaped by the *anamnesis* which forms the heart of its articulation (and so it is still seen as a 'wondering evocation') this development should perhaps be seen, not so much as an impoverishment, but rather as the acquisition of a characteristically christian emphasis in the prayer. For this suggestion, which does not materially

This second, and central, element in the prayer may be more or less protracted; whether or not it always makes explicit mention of all the major *mirabilia Dei*—in the orders of both creation and redemption—its proper object

> is much less the transient 'wonder' of a particular circumstance as perceived by the individual conscience, than the permanent and universal 'wonder' as perceived and remembered (hence the name of *anamnesis*) above all by the conscience of the community itself.[24]

Now it is clear that if this second section of the prayer were a mere recalling to mind of the mighty deeds which God had, in the past, performed for his people, then one could hardly account for the ecstatic declaration of praise and joy by this community, now. But, in fact,

> the statement of motive for blessing within a cultic action is a veritable kerygmatic annunciation to the assembly that this same *mirabile* is present here, active now, accomplishing its purpose still within the life of each and every member of the worshipping people.[25]

This is a point of fundamental importance for our theology of the eucharist, because it firmly situates the eucharistic prayer within the category of 'gospel', of

---

affect Fr Audet's thesis, nor my reliance on it, I am indebted to an unpublished paper by Fr J. D. Crichton.

[24] Audet, 19. Cf Kavanagh, 520.

[25] Kavanagh, 520. Maertens (112) goes so far as so say that: 'Le *mémorial* est l'essence même du culte chrétien et, en saine doctrine eucharistique, se trouve à la jonction du sens de l'action de grâces, du sacrifice et du sacrement.'

effective proclamation of the saving words of God to his people.[26] As such, it provides us with an essential insight towards an understanding of the relationship between that unique, unrepeatable, climactic, *mirabile Dei* which is the triumph of the cross, the sacrifice of Calvary, and the activity of the new people of God, assembled in the power of the Spirit of the risen Christ to celebrate that sacrifice. As Kavanagh puts it:

> This insight not only brings to light the actual indissolubility of the *kerygma* and the Christian *eucharistia*, but it also reveals the ideal balance that should obtain between the *kerygma*, baptism and Eucharist in all areas of Christian life and worship.[27]

By declaring the relationship between the present rite and the saving acts of God, the prayer makes the link between the *sacramentum tantum* and the *res et sacramentum* of the eucharist. It does more than that: it points beyond this link to the deeper level, to that shar-

[26] The fullest theological treatment known to me of this relationship between word and sacrament is an essay of Karl Rahner's: 'The Word and the Eucharist', in *Theological Investigations* IV (London 1966) 253–86. Cf also Audet, 27–30; Betz; Thurian, 64–7. James F. McCue ('Luther and Roman Catholicism on the Mass as Sacrifice', in *Journal of Ecumenical Studies* II, Duquesne 1965, 205–33) has some important remarks on the way in which the recovery of this dimension in our sacramental theology enables us to evaluate Luther's theology of the mass rather more positively than was previously possible. 'It is important, in a Catholic evaluation of Luther's conception of the mass, to point out that there is a substantial identity between the conception which Luther develops here of the relationship between sacrament (or sign) and faith and (for example) Karl Rahner's analysis of the relationship between *opus operatum* and *opus operantis*' (212; cf also 211, 216–17).

[27] Kavanagh, 528.

ing of life by men in God, begun already and to reach its consummation in the kingdom, which is the deep motive for our wonder and our praise.

> The 'final term' of the good news is a life of recon-
> ciliation, of integration between God and man as
> accomplished through the Son alone. It is the heart of
> the one great commandment he gave us, and it is—
> not fortuitously—what St Thomas calls the *res
> eucharistiae*.[28]

The third and final element in the prayer is

> the return of the initial 'benediction' by way of
> *inclusio*, or doxology, oftentimes coloured in different
> shades according to the particular theme which pre-
> vails in the anamnesis.[29]

Even from so brief a summary of the structure of a 'eucharist' as a literary form, it is not difficult to recog- nise that the three elements of the prayer are to be found in our present Roman canon: the initial 'blessing' in the dialogue before the preface, and the opening phrases of the prefaces themselves; the declaration of motive or *anamnesis* in the central passage of most of the prefaces and in the *Unde et memores*; the concluding 'blessing' in the final doxology to the canon. It is equally easy to see that, in the Roman canon, there are other, secondary elements which, not only quantitively but as a basis for theological reflection, have come to obscure the funda- mental form of the prayer.[30]

[28] Kavanagh, 527.
[29] Audet, 20. Cf Kavanagh, 521.
[30] '. . . emphases by other than primary elements have exerted pressure upon subsequent generations' understanding of the whole form of this type of prayer' (Kavanagh, 518). Later in the

article he insists that: 'The only proper methodology for solving this problem' (that of discovering the relationship between the various elements in our present canon, with a view to its reform) 'will be to keep in mind the primary structure-sequence of biblical *berakoth* and of the classic christian *eucharistia* developing from them' (3, where he rightly calls on *Liturgical Constitution* 24 in support of this claim). It is in this context that Fr Vagaggini's brilliant and timely study seems to me to be slightly defective. He says that 'The whole of the anaphora is essentially a hymn of rejoicing, thanksgiving, and supplication, but these characteristics ought to be particularly evident in the first part of the great prayer, the *eucharistia* par excellence. The second part is more directly sacrificial, containing as it must the institution, the anamnesis (the epiclesis, too, in my opinion), the offertory, the plea for a fruitful communion and the final doxology' (85; cf 91). This is unexceptionable, but it contains two latent weaknesses which become apparent in Fr Vagaggini's schematic breakdown of his own project for a reformed canon (cf 138). In the first place, what were formerly shifts of emphasis within an overarching 'eucharistic' unity ('the eucharistia *par excellence*' ... '*more directly* sacrificial') have here become virtually two distinct types of prayer. Thus he refers to the preface and its link-passage with the body of the prayer as 'the hymn of exaltation and thanksgiving for the economy of salvation', and to the rest of the canon as 'the sacrifice proper'. This is not simply a matter of typography, because it paves the way for the re-emergence of the current idea that 'praise' is not 'sacrifice', and 'sacrifice' is not 'praise': a dichotomy which he has himself already explicitly rejected. In the second place, by referring to one part of the body of the prayer as 'the' *anamnesis*, he obscures the fact that the preface itself and, indeed, the account of the institution, are parts of that general *anamnesis* which, we have seen, forms the central section in any true 'eucharist'. The first of these ambiguities, especially, is avoided, and the sense of the whole prayer is indicated, by Fr Kavanagh's fine statement: 'More is involved in "consecration" than the transformation of bread and wine into the sacramental body and blood of Christ. Considered liturgically, in terms of the whole eucharistic prayer, "consecration" is a processive offering to the Father of the whole assembly—Christ's body which is the Church' (6–7).

The most obvious instances of such secondary elements are the prayers of petition which abound in the Roman canon[31] and the *epiclesis* to which the eastern tradition, especially, attaches such importance.[32] The presence of these secondary elements is not surprising. To begin with, it is psychologically inevitable that the worshipping community, deeply orientated towards the future fulfilment of a reality which is now only present in sign, in pledge, in promise, should follow its ecstatic declaration of praise by an urgent expression of hope, of petition for the fulfilment of the promises. Such petitionary prayer is found in all christian *anaphoras* and, indeed, in several jewish *berakoth* as well.[33] Moreover, it seems probable that

the origin and development of the so-called 'epiclesis' are nothing else than particular episodes in this impressive rising of the *proseuchē* (prayers, properly so called) within the general equilibrium of the different

[31] 'On peut dire que, dès le 4e siècle, le canon romain a, pour ainsi dire, été invahi par l'idée d'oblation et la prière d'intercession' (B. Botte, 'Tradition Apostolique et Canon Romain', in *La Maison-Dieu* LXXXVII, 1966, 56).

[32] This is not to say that the epiclesis is unimportant (indeed, it seems reasonable to suggest that it is an essential element in the christian eucharist), but only to say that it is subordinate to the three primary elements of the prayer. Far from the explicit mention of the Spirit being unimportant, it is an inevitable concomitant of that trinitarian consciousness which will distinguish the christian 'eucharist' from its jewish antecedents. Perhaps we can say that the evocation of the Spirit is integral to christian praise, but that the invocation of the Spirit (insofar as this implies petitionary prayer) is, however important, a subsidiary element. (Cf John Meyendorff, 'Notes on the Orthodox Understanding of the Eucharist', in *Concilium* IV 3, 1967, 27-30.)

[33] Cf Audet, 31-2.

values of the *eucharistia*, as is already perceptible in the *Apostolic Tradition* of Hippolytus.[34]

It must be insisted once more, however, that these secondary elements in the *anaphora* must be kept as secondary: they must not be allowed, either in liturgical fact, or in theological theory, to obscure the basic characteristics of the prayer or of the action which it is concerned to interpret.[35]

From the point of view of theology, all these secondary elements may be situated in the context of the link between the present rite and the grace which it offers and promises; that is to say, they are all in some measure variants on the theme: 'Thy kingdom come'—'May they all be one, Father, may they be one in us, as you are in me and I am in you, so that the world may believe that it was you who sent me' (Jn 17.21).[36]

In view of its central importance in most theological discussion of the eucharist, it may seem surprising that no mention has yet been made of the narrative of institution. If one bears in mind what has been said already concerning the unity of the prayer, and its principal elements, then it obvious that the narrative belongs to the general category of *anamnesis* or statement of motive for the assembly's sacrifice of praise through the recalling of the *mirabilia Dei*.[37] Yet the precise relationship between this microcosm of the eucharistic liturgy and the

[34] Audet, 35.

[35] Cf Audet, 32.

[36] Cf Thurian, 67–75, 106.

[37] As is indicated by the inclusion, at this point, of the command: 'As often as you shall do these things, you shall do them in *anamnesis*.'

rest of the prayer in which, in most liturgies, it is set constitutes one of the thorniest problems in liturgical history.[38] The most satisfactory solution, the justification of which is impossible here, is that a sound christian instinct led the church to formulate the reference to the last supper within its eucharistic prayer in narrative form; that precisely because, as a narrative, it was something of a 'foreign body' so far as the major rhythms of the prayer were concerned, its place in the prayer varied from one liturgy to another; that its inclusion in this form was possible (psychologically and culturally speaking) because there was jewish precedent for the inclusion of such narrative material within the texture of a *berakah*.[39]

[38] 'Ainsi posée, la question est limitée au canon ou anaphore. Etendue à l'ensemble de la messe depuis l'offertoire, elle aurait été apparement plus simple: il aurait suffit de rappeler que les quatre gestes de Jésus prenant le pain, rendant grâces, rompant et distribuant, sont repris dans les quatre temps de la messe, offertoire, canon, fraction et communion. Mais le vrai problème est précisément dans le canon. Pour sa part, en effet, *cette partie de la messe ne répond qu'au seul rite de la bénédiction*; les trois autres gestes de Jésus—offrande, fraction et communion—lui sont extérieurs; neanmoins le canon contient à l'intérieur de sa bénédiction le récit institutionnel, lequel commémore précisément tous les actes du Christ, y compris la bénédiction qu'il est. On voit la difficulté' (Ligier, 26; cf above 67–8). It is undoubtedly true that the presence of this 'verbal microcosm' of the whole eucharistic liturgy in the centre of the *anaphora* has been a prime factor in distracting the attention of theologians from the whole rite as the basis for their reflections.

[39] This is the thesis of Ligier's article, just cited. It is not the inclusion in the christian prayer of our Lord's words over the bread and cup that creates the problem: it is their inclusion, together with details of his gestures and of his 'rubrical directives' to the apostles, in narrative form, in a prayer whose structure does not lead one to expect the inclusion of such material. The

4+

So far it has been asserted that the meaning of the mass, as of any other sacrament, is determined by its *forma*, by the words which declare the christian significance of the gesture being enacted. It has been further asserted that the *forma* of the mass, the *anaphora*, is of the literary genre of the jewish *berakah*, or wondering evocation, in praise and proclamation, of the mighty deeds of God, a praise motivated by the conviction that the victory of the cross, to be consummated in the brotherhood of the kingdom, is effectively shown forth and made present even in this brotherhood of the worshipping assembly. These two assertions, taken together, lead to the conclusion that the answer to the question 'how do christians offer sacrifice?' is: by celebrating a eucharist, a *sacrificium laudis*,[40] in the form of a fraternal meal which expresses and deepens their commitment of faith to God in Christ by expressing and deepening their commitment to the brotherhood of the kingdom. The principal agent in this celebration is Christ, because the praise and commitment of the people is the praise and commitment of Christ; the prayer of the president who voices the assembly's covenant-accepting praise and faith

---

problem has been well put by Dr Mascall: 'The point which is of primary importance for our present purpose is—that what Christ commanded was that they should do this for his *anamnesis*, not that they should *say* that they were doing it' (*Corpus Christi* London 1965, 58, where he also quotes a remark of Fr Benoit's: 'On ne récite pas une rubrique, on l'exécute').

[40] '... we easily understand, so it seems to me, that the *eucharistia* should have appeared, in the first place, very exactly as is suggested by the name it finally retained: a "sacrifice of praise" ' (Audet, 28).

is the prayer of Christ, and the food which they share as the language of their brotherhood is the body of Christ.[41]

Merely to make such assertions, however, is simply to shout across the gulf which today separates Roman catholic theologies of the mass. It sounds so unlike what many people would recognise as a 'truly catholic' theology that some attempt must be made to show how, within a common faith, two such different languages articulating that faith can have arisen.[42] The simplest way to do this seems to be by means of a summary (necessarily drawn with very broad strokes of the brush) of the way in which, in the course of twenty centuries, the languages used in connection with the mass have developed. It was stated earlier that the way in which we talk about a thing depends upon the image of that thing which we have in mind. In what follows, then, it will be suggested that the variations in the language of eucharistic theology can be accounted for by observing how what we earlier referred to as the dominant image for this theology has been far from constant. If, however, the central argument of this chapter is sound, then the fact that images other than that of the 'table-fellowship

---

[41] 'To accomplish so great a work, Christ is always present in his Church. . . . He is present in the sacrifice of the mass, not only in the person of his minister, "the same now offering, through the ministry of priests, who formerly offered himself on the cross", but especially under the eucharistic species. . . . He is present in his words. . . . He is present, lastly, when the Church prays and sings, for he promised: "Where two or three are gathered together in my name, there am I in the midst of them" (Mt 18.20)' (*Constitution on Liturgy* 7; for further commentary on this article, cf ch 5).

[42] In the following chapter, I shall try to say something further about the relationship between these two languages.

of the brotherhood of the new covenant' have been employed, from time to time, as the basis for theological reflection, cannot be taken as an excuse for what, in terms of the principles of sacramental theology, must be regarded as something less than perfect fidelity to the demands of the apostolic tradition.

It must also be pointed out that propositions formulated within different theological languages (articulating the significance of different dominant images) cannot be held to contradict each other merely because the terms employed are different in each case. One has first to learn 'the rules of the game', and to discover the function of a particular proposition within the language in which it is being employed. Then, and only then, is one in a position to interpret the statement in terms of some other theological language.[43]

[43] These considerations are of considerable importance if one is going to discover what, for example, was being affirmed or denied in the theological disputes of the sixteenth century. McCue (207) asks: 'What sort of disagreement is involved when one man or community says, "The mass is a sacrifice", while another says, "The mass is not a sacrifice"?', and later on he comments: 'We shall have to attempt to articulate Luther's understanding of what the mass *is*, and shall try to relate this to the Roman Catholic understanding of the sacrificial character of the mass' (208). The problem is, of course, of far wider interest than mere historical exegesis: 'For example, what did St Paul write to the Corinthians and what meaning does it have for us? What did the Council of Trent say about the eucharist in the context of the questions being asked at that time, and what does it mean for us today? I will call the explanation relative to the first situation a "commentary", and that relative to our situation an "interpretation". Commentary and interpretation are both needed; together they compose the whole of theology. . . . A *commentary* serves first of all to facilitate a good understanding of a dogma. . . . The *interpretation* of a dogma in the context of

Perhaps the most obvious fact about the eucharist as celebrated in the first three centuries was that it was the act of a community, of a brotherhood, and that the participants were directly and primarily conscious of this fact. In other words, they came together as brothers, in order to express and deepen their brotherhood *in Christo*; they did not come together in one place to perform some function not directly related to the brotherhood. The point is an important one. The members of a theatre club may come together, in virtue of their common membership of the club, in order to do something which could be done, quite satisfactorily, by a reduced number, or even by a single individual: namely, to watch a play. The guests at a dinner-party, on the other hand, come together, in virtue of their common invitation, precisely to do something together. If none of the guests turned up, the host might eat the supper on his own, sorrowfully toasting 'absent friends', but this would be a seriously diminished, although not altogether meaningless activity that could only by a stretch of the imagination be described as 'having a dinner-party'.

---

the twentieth century is even more difficult. Such an interpretation first requires a comparison of two contexts of history and language—that in which the text was originally located and that in which we live. Only when such a comparative study has been made can we attempt to "translate" the ancient dogma into the context in which we are situated. In this process it can happen that key words of a dogma will be replaced in the "translation" by others, or will not appear at all, because words in diverse contexts acquire diverse meanings. The "translation" of a dogma can therefore involve considerable verbal change' (Piet Schoonenberg, quoted by *Herder Correspondence* IV Dublin, March 1967, 95). Cf an essay of mine, 'Dogmas and Doctrinal Process', in *Until He Comes* (Dayton 1968, pp. 3–33).

In the case of the theatre-club, the members assemble, in virtue of their common membership, to perform a function in common, but the object of their individual concern is what happens on the stage. In the case of the dinner-party, however, the members assemble, in virtue of their common invitation, to perform a function in common, and the object of their concern is each other. These two images (which, like all analogies, should not be pressed too far: they are intended as parables, not allegories) illustrate two very different ways in which a group of people may be said to be 'doing something together'. Whatever may turn out to be the case at later periods in the church's history, there is no doubt but that the celebration of the eucharist in the early church belonged to the dinner-party, rather than to the theatre-club, category of communal activities.

The context of their gathering was their fellowship *in Christo*, their common expectancy of the kingdom (as the achievement of human brotherhood in the love of God), their common relationship in the Spirit of him who the Father had raised from the dead. The action of God in Christ was, in their consciousness, the high-point of the mighty works of God for his people; their action, therefore, and the prayer which declared the meaning of the action, was a recalling of this mighty work (and, often, of the series of mighty works which had preceded it).[44] But their consciousness of being together in Christ

[44] Cf the outline of the early development of the eucharist in Jungmann, *Missarum Sollemnia* I, 33–46, particularly 'Célébrer en un repas sacré le souvenir du Seigneur, de sa Passion rédemptrice, tel fut le motif fondamental et originel: l'aspect de repas est au premier plan au début.... L'idée de l'union au Christ glorieux domine la conscience, en même temps que se

meant that they were deeply alive to the fact that the existence of their brotherhood and, in particular, of this act of brotherhood which was their present assembly, was also a mighty work of God; that they were included, by God, in that climatic work which he had wrought in Christ. Their common action, therefore, and the prayer which articulated it, was a true 'eucharist'.[45]

Between the third and fifth centuries, although the basic elements in the celebration remained unchanged, both in fact and in the consciousness of the worshipping assembly, there was a perceptible shift of emphasis. What happened was that the church came to reflect more deeply on the significance of this action which it performed. She became reflexively more conscious of the fact that the meaning of this cultic fraternal meal which she celebrated was, indeed, the whole meaning of the church. And the meaning of the church is the progressive incorporation of mankind into the paschal mystery,

---

manifeste concrètement l'union des fidèles entre eux.... Et si déjà, dans le milieu ou vivait l'Église primitive, outre diverses formules de bénédictions, la prière d'action de grâces s'ajoutait à chaque repas, combien plus encore à celui-ci' (44).

[45] A classic description of the early eucharist, of course, is that found in Justin's *First Apology* (c 150 AD): 'At the conclusion of the prayers, we greet one another with a kiss. Then bread and a chalice containing wine mixed with water are presented to the one presiding over the brethren. He takes them and offers praise and glory to the Father of all, through the name of the Son and of the Holy Spirit, and he recites lengthy prayers of "eucharist" to God in the name of those to whom he granted such favours. At the end of these prayers and "eucharist", all present express their approval by saying "Amen".... And when he who presides has "made eucharist", they whom we call deacons permit each one present to partake of the "eucharistized" bread, and wine and water; and they carry it also to the absentees.'

into the death and resurrection of Jesus Christ. With this deeper reflexive awareness there came a more ample use of sacrificial terminology in the *anaphoras* themselves, and in christian preaching and writing concerning the eucharist. The concept of sacrifice had, from the very beginning, been applied to the death and resurrection of Christ, but now it began to be applied with greater insistence than before to the life and actions of the new people, the people who live, work, and pray *in Christo*.[46] Thus it is that the table round which they gathered came to be described, metaphorically, as an 'altar',[47] and that the great eucharistic prayer which, at least so far as the Roman canon is concerned, more or less reached its final form towards the end of this period,

---

[46] In view of the fact that the christians of the first three centuries only employed the language of sacrifice in order strenuously to reject the idea that altars, temples, victims, and so on, had any place in christian worship (cf *Missarum Sollemnia* 1, 49), it is somewhat superficial to see in this rejection simply a desire to avoid confusing the eucharist with pagan cult. Their intention was positive: to insist that there was now no longer any need for these things, because there was born a brotherhood in the Spirit whose access to God in Christ made it possible for human commitment, love, service, self-sacrifice, to contain and express a relationship to God which could earlier only be pointed to, symbolised, by the ritual use of material objects.

[47] According to Thurian (57), Cyprian was the first person to apply the term 'altar' to the table of the eucharist. If we are going to avoid being anachronistic, it is necessary to read the texts of this (or any other period) in the light of what was actually going on in the assembly. Already, for St Paul, the eucharist could be described as a sacrificial meal (cf 1 Cor 10.18). But the altar in respect of which, for Paul, the eucharist (the whole eucharist: taking, blessing, breaking, and eating) was a 'communion' was the cross.

came to include a wealth of specifically sacrificial terminology.[48] Moreover, since the church was now living in a culture other than that of her origins, it is hardly surprising that there should have been some shift in the importance which was attached to the various elements in the *anaphora*. Thus, for example, greater significance came to be attached to the petitionary elements in the prayer.

The liturgical practice of the period, however, and the writings of the fathers bear ample witness to the fact that the more explicit recognition of the sacrificial nature of the christian eucharist did not involve any diminution either in the understanding of the sufficiency of Christ's sacrifice, or of its unrepeatable nature, or of the radically new, and totally 'spiritual'[49] nature of christian worship. The application of sacrificial terminology to christian worship was not made in distinction from the act of God in Christ, but from a profound realisation of their identity.

The church, then, celebrated its family meal, celebrated and deepened its community-situation *in Christo*, and understood that celebration as an act of involvement

[48] A weakness of some latin theology has been to write too exclusively within the theological perspectives of the Roman canon, which is, in many ways, a-typical. So, for example, while it is true that any developed *anaphora* contains a wealth of explicitly sacrificial terminology, it is also generally agreed that the Roman canon displays an over-preoccupation with the idea of 'oblation', at the cost of overshadowing the dominantly 'eucharistic' note maintained in many other *anaphoras* of the same period (cf the greek Alexandrine *anaphora* of St Basil, the text of which may be found in Vagaggini, 51–8).

[49] Which does not, of course, mean 'disincarnate', but fully personal in the Spirit of the risen Christ.

4*

in the sacrificial death and resurrection of Jesus Christ. Christ the priest, who had created this assembly, the church, in the gift of his Spirit, enabled this to be the case; Christ the victim, in whom this assembly lived, enabled their self-gift, their commitment in praise to the covenant-will of God, to be his self-gift, his commitment to his Father's will.

For the christian of the fifth century, the dominant image (sign, symbol) in which the sacrifice of Christ was celebrated was still the three-dimensional concrete image of the actual assembly itself; of a people taking, blessing, sharing and consuming food and drink. This was the ritual sacrifice of the new people; the *sacrificium laudis*, the praise of a people dedicated to God in each other; the 'spiritual sacrifice' of personal commitment to brotherhood in the Spirit of the risen Christ.

However, just as the author of the Letter to the Hebrews had drawn on the imagery of old testament temple sacrifices in order to apply the concept of sacrifice to the humiliation of penal murder and to the glory of new life in the Spirit, so now, for the church as it celebrated her eucharist, there hovered at the back of the mind the image of those bloody sacrifices whose meaning it had pondered in order to interpret, in their light, its own radically different form of religious activity.

So long as the liturgical assembly was living out, in personally expressive dramatic action, the imagery of the supper, then this remained, correctly, the dominant image for theological reflection. The christian consciousness was not distorted by the contrapuntal imagery of pre-christian sacrificial forms. No harm was done by referring to the table as an 'altar', to the presiding minister as a 'priest', to the bread and cup as a 'sacrificial offering'. The imagery of earlier, pre-christian forms of sacrifice and priesthood remained secondary and subordinated.[50]

If, however, we move on a few hundred years, into the high Middle Ages, the picture becomes rather darker. Now we find that the living assembly has withered away, the mass has ceased, to all appearances, to be the celebration of the last supper by God's holy people, gathered together to express and deepen their brotherhood *in Christo*. The people have, because of the language-barrier and the increasing clericalisation of ecclesiastical structures, been effectively excluded from

[50] Whatever may have been the case in regard to jewish liturgical theology (and the received view that they understood 'sacrifice' and 'meal' as consecutive events of distinct theological significance has been called in question—cf Louis Bouyer *Rite and Man* London 1963; Hans Joachim Kraus *Worship in Israel* Oxford 1966, 112–24), to claim that, in the celebration of the eucharist, the eating of the meal means one thing ('communion in the sacrifice'), and the eucharistic prayer another ('offering the sacrifice'), is to deny those fundamental principles of sacramental theology on which this chapter is based. In other words, if the purpose of the *forma sacramenti* is to declare the meaning of the gesture, the rite, in which it is set, then to say (as is done as early as Hippolytus) 'we offer this cup', is not to describe something that happens before the cup is shared, but is to say that the sharing of the cup (the gesture) is meaningfully described as an act of offering (ie the celebration of this meal is declared to be the offering of a sacrifice). If what is actually going on is the sharing of a sacred meal, then it is healthy and valuable to declare that the meaning of this meal is the offering of christian sacrifice. In other words, writing in a period of lively liturgical participation, Cyprian could not mean that 'this is a table and an altar' (as if it were an object with two distinct uses); he could only mean that as a table, as the focus of our meal-gathering, it is an altar, because our meal-gathering is our sacrifice.

the celebration.[51] Instead of doing something, they now watch somebody else doing something 'over there', in the sanctuary.[52] In other words, in terms of the categories which I employed at the beginning of this section, the mass now belongs to the theatre-club, rather than to the dinner-party type of communal gathering. The christian brotherhood has been reduced in fact (and, therefore, rapidly, in theory also) to the pre-christian situation in which the common herd stood afar off, while the 'holy men', the cultic officials, carried out the acts of ritual worship.[53]

The concrete image, the existential sign, no longer bears any relation to the fraternal meal: it is now a crowd of people watching someone else at work. Therefore, hardly surprisingly, the image of the supper ceases to be the dominant image in subordination to which other,

[51] 'La deviation menaçante était celle qui provient, à toutes les epoques, de la rarefaction de la communion, seul rite laic à la fois parfaitement communautaire et parfaitement personnel. *L'histoire de la messe tourne autour de l'histoire de cette participation directe et unanime aux mystères*' (Denis-Boulet, 278; my stress).

[52] 'On ne s'occupe plus de la participation de l'assistance au sacrifice du Christ ... La messe devient de plus en plus mystère de la descente divine, on l'admire et on la contemple de loin' (Jungmann *Missarum Sollemnia* I, 117).

[53] 'Le prêtre seul peut entrer dans ce sanctuaire, tandis que le peuple, comme jadis lors du sacrifice de Zacharie, se tient dehors, attend et prie' (*Missarum Sollemnia* I, 115; cf III, 48). An eloquent illustration of this is the insertion of 'pro quibus tibi offerimus' into the canon: medieval eucharistic theory and practice was so deficient that: 'L'on s'étonne en effet qu'on puisse dire des fidèles ... "qui tibi offerunt hoc sacrificium laudis" ' (*Missarum Sollemnia* I, 116), so the text was 'improved'. Perhaps the most serious evidence of the decline is that it is now a place, and not a people, which is regarded as the 'sanctuary of God'.

secondary images may safely be employed. It is now a matter of touch-and-go which of three possible images (the meal, the temple sacrifice, the death of Christ) is the primary one in terms of which the meaning of the action will be interpreted. It is hardly surprising, in view of the total dependence, in any orthodox theology of the mass on Calvary, that it is the image of Calvary which wins; Calvary, moreover, interpreted in its turn according to the pre-christian imagery of temple sacrifice. The slightest movement of the celebrant is now understood as a dramatic enactment of some moment in the passion and death of Christ. The strong identity of the all-inclusive historical event of the death of Christ and the new life of the brotherhood *in Christo*, although continually affirmed in theory, became increasingly difficult to relate in practice to what was actually going on. The withering away of the living, communicating assembly had its theoretical counterpart in the loss of a strong doctrine of sacramentality. The 'sign' of Christ's sacrifice is no longer seen as the worshipping assembly in the act of the covenant-supper, but is sought for in pictures[54] which have an existence independent of the people in whom Christ exercises his priesthood. The mood of the mass is less and less one of joyful wonder, of celebration, of 'eucharist'; it is, especially under gallican influence, rather one of timorous petition, of fear and uncertainty, almost as if God had not, in Christ, spoken his definitive, irrevocable word of forgiveness.[55]

[54] For example, the sacrificial nature of the mass is supposed to be shown forth by the separation of the two consecrations, a theory described by Vagaggini as an 'explanation of medieval origin' (102; cf above, ch 2, p 48).

[55] Jungmann (*Missarum Sollemnia* III, 294) has traced the in-

The transposition of imagery which led to this distortion and lack of balance wrought particular havoc with the understanding of the *anaphora*. It ceased to be understood as a benediction, a proclamation, a 'eucharist'.[56] It became instead the mystic context in which the consecration of the bread and wine took place. In place of the *sacrificium laudis*, of the praise of a people wonderingly grateful for their call to the kingdom, the *anaphora* and in particular the narrative of the institution was thought of only too often in a way which, quite frankly, had overtones of the magical.[57]

This was the situation which confronted the reforming spirits of the sixteenth century. Valiant efforts were made, by the leaders of the protestant reform and by the fathers of the Council of Trent, to reshape both the celebration itself, and the theory according to which it was interpreted. The dead weight of history was, inevitably, too strong for them; their considerable success was

---

fluence of arianism on the decline in frequent communion. In the same way, it can hardly be doubted that, in practice, a broadly monophysite tendency led to a not completely satisfactory understanding of the sense in which the ordained minister could be called a 'mediator' (cf R. Salaün and E. Marcus, *Qu'est-ce qu'un prêtre?* Paris 1965, 88–94).

[56] Even those theologians who tried to replace the jungle of allegorisation with some ordered theological interpretation of the mass were often agreed that the preface was a concluding prayer to the first part of the mass (cf *Missarum Sollemnia* I, 152).

[57] 'Words, real words, which make sense and are spoken with this intent, disappeared from the worship or no longer played an essential role in it. Even in its formulas, worship tended to be no more than a purely ritualistic action. But by the same token, the ritualistic action became dehumanised; and, like it or not, it ceased at the same time to be really religious' (Bouyer, *Rite and Man*, 58–9).

doomed to be a partial failure.[58] In the catholic church, the worst abuses were corrected but, partly because polemical bias prevented the vernacularisation of the liturgy, the attempt of Trent to reintroduce frequent communion failed, and the celebration of the eucharist remained a clerical, non-communitarian affair. The theatre-club held the field, and reached a fresh expression in the baroque theology of the liturgy as the court ceremonial of a people dancing attendance on the divine *roi soleil*.[59] In the protestant churches, in spite of many excellent reforms of both theology and liturgical practice, polemical bias prevented a balanced recovery of the primitive reality.[60] Not only was the concept of sacri-

[58] If one reads only the canons of Trent on the sacrificial nature of the mass (Denzinger 948–56), one might get the impression of a distinctly imbalanced eucharistic doctrine. But the canons are concerned precisely to affirm those points of doctrine rejected by the reformers. If, on the other hand, one reads the text of the decree (Denzinger 937a–46), one cannot fail but be struck by its remarkable balance: a balance not always preserved in post-tridentine theology. It is, of course, true that both Trent and the reformers were rendered incapable, by the dialectic of dissent, of adequately integrating each other's positive doctrinal and pastoral insights into their systems.

[59] Cf Bouyer, *Life and Liturgy* (London 1962) 2–9.

[60] 'If the mass is essentially the reception in faith of the forgiveness of sins promised at the Last Supper and won on Calvary, then it is, Luther charges, a basic distortion to make the mass something we offer to God. If the mass is a receiving it is not a giving, if it is a testament it is not a sacrifice. Making of the mass a sacrifice of this sort denies two basic facts about the christian life: it is God who gives to us; we have nothing to give and can thus only receive. It is here that Luther's general thesis on the relations of grace, faith, and works shapes his understanding of the mass. He attacks "sacrifice" as synonymous with "work". The dichotomy between giving and receiving is insisted upon uncompromisingly' (McCue, 217).

fice too often considered as standing in necessary opposition to the concept of the Lord's supper,[61] but defective theologies of justification and grace prevented the rebirth of a strong doctrine of *anamnesis*, of the celebration of brotherhood *in Christo*.[62] While the catholic church retained its conviction that the weekly eucharist was central to the church's life (but failed to celebrate it as an act of the church), the protestant churches recovered a sense of celebration but, in practice, failed to

[61] A calmer evaluation of reformation teaching is leading catholics to a better understanding of what was not being denied by the great reformers. It was, after all, Luther who wrote: 'To be sure this sacrifice of prayer, praise, and thanksgiving and of ourselves as well, we are not to present before God in our own person. But we are to lay it upon Christ and let him present it for us. . . . From these words (ie Heb 9.24 and Rom 8.34) we learn that we do not offer Christ as a sacrifice, but that Christ offers us. And in this way it is permissible, yes, profitable, to call the mass a sacrifice; not on its own account, but because we offer ourselves as a sacrifice along with Christ. That is, we lay ourselves on Christ by a firm faith in his testament and do not otherwise appear before God with our prayer, praise, and sacrifice except through Christ and his mediation. Nor do we doubt that Christ is our priest or minister in heaven before God. Such faith, truly, brings it to pass that Christ takes up our cause, presents us and our prayer and praise, and also offers himself for us in heaven. If the mass were so understood and for this reason called a sacrifice, it would be well' (*A Treatise on the New Testament*, quoted by McCue, 218).

[62] Neither catholic nor reformed liturgical piety really succeeded in breaking out of the smothering individualism which had distorted the essentially ecclesial (communitarian) nature of the eucharist. Is it too far-fetched to see a marked similarity in structure between that strain of evangelical piety which concentrates on the relationship between the individual believer and Jesus, and that strain of catholic piety which finds the activity of other people at mass (and especially singing during communion) a 'distraction from prayer'?

recapture the conviction of its centrality as the focal act of christian worship. There is, so far as I know, little evidence that an adequate understanding of the literary genre of the critical element in the celebration, the *forma sacramenti*, the great eucharistic prayer, played a significant part in the reform movement anywhere in Europe.

In the years before the second world war, the liturgical movement had outgrown its romantic origins and become uncompromisingly pastoral in orientation. Thanks to the work of pioneers in this field such as Romano Guardini and Pius Parsch, the nature of the eucharist as essentially the expression and source of christian communion was again being strongly recovered. Frequent communion, so strongly urged by St Pius x, was ceasing to be the individual devotion of the inordinately pious, and becoming once again the strongest expression of christian brotherhood. But this development, whose sources lay in biblical and historical research and an increasing awareness of pastoral needs, was insufficiently integrated with dogmatic theology, which was still employing as its dominant image that of pre-christian sacrifice, and was still primarily concerned with understanding the mass as truly the sacrifice of Christ. In view of the fact that, in terms of liturgical experience, the christian image of sacrifice (the 'brotherhood-meal of the new covenant') was, in the consciousness of worshippers, acquiring once again its proper priority, some considerable tension between these two claimants to the title of dominant image was inevitable. In the early days of the liturgical movement, it was necessary to stress the fact that the eucharist was 'also' the sacrifice of the church because, in spite of the strongly sacrificial language of catholic theology (which language was referred only to the *actio Christi*, and not to the action of the people in Christ), many of the devout still saw the mass as a complex ritual machinery for achieving the real presence. But the persisting failure (in spite of the valuable contribution made by Dom Odo Casel and the mystery-presence school) to formulate adequately the crucial questions of the relationship of the past deed of Christ to the present action of his brethren, and of the relationship, within the eucharist, between the *actio Christi* and the action of the people, can still be traced to a failure to advert to the principles of sacramental theology outlined at the beginning of this chapter.[63] In view of this failure to ask the correct methodological questions about the relationship of image to meaning in eucharistic theology, even those notable syntheses which appeared at this period, refusing the alternatives of either meal or sacrifice, tended, at least at the popular level, to become compromises which sidestepped the central issue.

The compromise usually took the form of claiming that the canon of the mass, the *anaphora*, was the 'moment' of sacrifice, and the actual sharing of the consecrated bread and wine was the 'communion in the sacrifice'.[64] Consciously or unconsciously, the dominant

[63] This failure is strikingly apparent in the custom of referring to 'The mass and the sacraments' (as if the mass were not itself a sacrament), or in the division of the tract on the eucharist in manuals of theology into 'the eucharist as sacrifice' and 'the eucharist as sacrament'.

[64] This, of course, is the picture employed in *Mediator Dei* (cf § 122, in the CTS edition).

image that underlies such an interpretation is still that of the pre-christian temple sacrifice.[65] The one question that was not asked with sufficient seriousness was 'what is the canon of the mass, and therefore what can the assembled people be said to be 'doing' during the canon?[66]

Before the second world war, all the elements of a renewed and synthesised understanding of the eucharist can be found in the writings of liturgical theologians, but these elements tended to exist in an independent and uncoordinated manner. The necessary catalyst that could fuse them into a vision of the eucharist at once astoundingly simple and profoundly mysterious was still lacking. The catalyst, of course, was not the theoretical insights of some master theologian, but the recovery of christian experience through a renewal of the liturgical community. Studying the indispensable but scattered insights of the liturgists and theologians of the first half of this century, a spectator might have been forgiven for asking 'can these bones live?' Pius xii's encyclical *Mediator Dei*, in so many ways a child of its time, began to provide an answer by putting the papal authority squarely behind the accelerating momentum of the liturgical movement. The spirit began to gather the bones together, and to breathe life into the worship of the christian people. The Vatican Council's *Constitution on the Liturgy* is the formal expression of the new life pul-

[65] And, moreover, of pre-christian sacrifice as seen in the light of one particular, and not totally satisfactory interpretation (cf note 50 above). To question the suitability of this image is not to question the doctrinal assertions formulated in its light (cf above, ch 2).

[66] Until, perhaps, the landmark of Dom Gregory Dix's *The Shape of the Liturgy* (London 1945).

sating in the body that was not dead, but sleeping, and is the programme for future pastoral reform and theological development.

It would, of course, be incorrect to describe the present tensions in eucharistic theology as if there were two groups of people, each dedicated to a different dominant image, and a different methodology, in their theology of the eucharist. It is rather the case that, as the fruits of biblical and historical research are harvested in a more authentic experience of the mass as the central act of christian brotherhood, the 'battle of the dominant image' is currently being waged within the consciousness of the individual christian. In view of the fact that it is the same people, very often, who instinctively employ the imagery of the solomonic temple, while increasingly living the imagery of the christian assembly, it is hardly surprising that one should often be able to detect a tendency, in the statements of preachers and theologians, to oscillate uneasily between two theological languages whose relationship has not been clearly grasped.[67]

The tenacity with which the pre-christian imagery refuses to relinquish its grip is accountable for by the inertia of history and by the fear that to opt clearly for the methodology proposed in this chapter would be to deny, in some way, those doctrinal insights acquired by the church during a period in its history in which, inevitably, it expressed them in a manner calculated to obscure the uniqueness and originality of the christian religious situation. This fear will only finally be exor-

[67] Illustration of the prevalent unclarity is probably unnecessary, but it can be seen, for example, even in Fr Jungmann's good little book, *The Eucharistic Prayer* (London 1966; cf 19–20, 36).

cised when a simplified *anaphora*, a prayer reformed according to the model of the *berakah* from which it sprang, but which yet, in its language, bears explicit witness to our contemporary understanding of christianity is, once again, intelligibly proclaimed in the assembly.[68] Then, and only then, will it clearly be seen that the dominant image for eucharistic theology must be the image of that concrete, living institution which the Lord left to his church for its *anamnesis* of him. Then, and only then, will it be easily accepted that the proud title 'eucharistic sacrifice' does adequately describe how it is that the pilgrim church experiences and shares, in the sign of brotherhood in the love of God, the climactic event of human history, the victory of the cross of Christ.

[68] It is urgently necessary that the preparation for this reform should be undertaken without delay, for, as Fr McManus says in his introduction to Fr Vagaggini's book: 'In the English-speaking world, with some notable exceptions, discussion of the reform of the Roman canon has been negligible. The lesson of the immediate past has not been learned. Bishops, priests, and teachers have been giving assurances for two or three decades now that liturgical changes are impossible or unlikely. Everything, from the introduction of the vernacular to the eucharist facing the people has been decried. And every such assurance has proved false' (in Vagaggini, 9). And, even in such discussion as there has been, there is little evidence that the theological shift which both demands this reform, and which will flourish as a result of it, has been sufficiently adverted to. I have written this chapter as a contribution to this discussion.

4
Whose sacrifice?

That the Mass is truly a sacrifice, drawing its sacrificial efficacy wholly from the redemptive sacrifice of Christ, has always been maintained in Catholic theology; but the question of *how* it is a sacrifice is one that is open to further investigations.[1]

I believe that the sort of answer one gives to that question (let us call it the 'how' question) will depend on which of the two theological methods, outlined at the beginning of the previous chapter, one adopts. I have already hinted, in chapter 2, at the way in which I should want to try to answer the 'how' question, and some of the elements of this answer are to be found, here and there, in chapter 3. For the sake of clarity, however, it may be useful to collect them together and so to attempt to formulate this answer, somewhat schematically, in greater detail. In this chapter, therefore, I shall first try to answer the 'how' question; I shall then sug-

[1] Francis Clark sj *Eucharistic Sacrifice and the Reformation* (London 1960) 96–7.

gest that the answer given does full justice to the demands made upon the catholic theologian by the dogmatic statements of the Council of Trent; finally I shall say something about the ecumenical importance of this problem.

The 'how' question, for all its apparent innocence, masks the far more difficult question: whose sacrifice is the mass?

> What is so striking is that the Mass appears in our liturgy at once and before all else as *our* sacrifice, and so it appears throughout: *we* bring gifts, *we* beg for acceptance, *we* prepare *my* sacrifice and *your* sacrifice. On the other hand we are accustomed from the side of dogmatic theology to regard the Mass just as precisely and almost exclusively as the sacrifice of Christ. The fact that *we* are offering is scarcely mentioned in theological discussions. The only topics discussed are the fact that Christ offers; enquiry is made as to how he offers, how he renews his sacrifice or makes it present, whether any destruction takes place or not. Even catechisms employ the same methods of consideration.[2]

That passage indicates very clearly that the 'apparently obvious' answer to the 'whose sacrifice?' question depends, once again, upon which of the two theological methods one employs (for, as a matter of fact, the sort of dogmatic theology to which Fr Jungmann refers, and which for too long has held the field, almost invariably adopts that conceptualist, non-historical, and a-priori

[2] Josef Jungmann *The Eucharistic Prayer* (London 1966) 14.

method which, in these chapters, I have tried to avoid).[3] It also suggests that the 'whose sacrifice?' question cannot be answered until we have agreed upon the way in which the relationship between Christ and his church is to be understood. Is it the case that the church is a community of people who, at any given moment, pre-exist the presence of Christ in their midst, or is it rather the case that the presence of Christ pre-exists, and is the essential precondition for, the existence and activity of that group of people whom we call the church?

Questions concerning the presence of Christ are never simply questions of the 'is he there or is he not?' variety. The extent to which persons are present to each other as persons depends upon the type and quality of the relationship between them. Mere physical proximity, for example, of one human being to another does not constitute personal presence.[4] It should be obvious that whereas two human beings can be sub-personally pre-

[3] The two methods have been well, if slightly polemically, contrasted by Michael Novak in *The Open Church* (London 1964) 52–70. I intend the term 'non-historical' to have the sense which Novak gives it in those pages. In the matter of the mass, of course, this approach to theology has been rendered especially unhelpful by those polemical shifts of emphasis to which all controversial theology (once it concentrates on 'answering the adversary', rather than examining the facts) is subject.

[4] The term 'presence' is notoriously slippery, and I shall discuss it again in the next chapter. Many of the problems that arise in connection with its use are epistemological, rather than strictly doctrinal. Not a little of the writing on the eucharist seems to take it as axiomatic that the correct model for the presence of Christ is the local, physical juxtaposition of inanimate objects. This assumption must clearly be questioned, both on philosophical grounds (we are, after all, talking about the mutual presence of persons), and on theological ones (we are talking about sacramental presence, presence 'in the order of sign').

sent to each other (one has only to think of a tube-train in the rush hour), this sort of presence is irrelevant to any consideration of the presence of Christ in the church. If I am sub-personally present to someone else, present simply in my bodiliness, this is due to a failure (which does not necessarily imply moral guilt) to raise that presence to the human, the personal level. After all I could, if I wanted to, turn to the other man in the tube, ask after his health, offer him a cigarette, enquire about the wife and kids, and generally take a personal interest in him. Now to suggest that Christ could be present to his church sub-personally would be to suggest that, at that moment, Christ did not take an interest in, did not personally care about us—which would be blasphemous. Therefore if Christ is present to a group of people, he is personally present, actively caring for and concerned about these people.

The next stage in the argument is to notice that a personal relationship (presence) between people cannot be achieved 'silently', without communication. Persons become present to each other by disclosing, in word and gesture, that care and concern for each other which constitutes their mutual presence as personal. Therefore if Christ is present to a group of people, his presence is achieved in the very act of disclosure; it does not pre-exist this disclosure as 'merely bodily', or sub-personal presence. Christ is 'here' because he speaks to us, in his speaking to us; he is not first 'simply here' so that he can (as a consequence) speak to us.[5]

---

[5] '. . . the first truth of the eucharistic doctrine is "This is my body", not, "Here I am present" ' (Karl Rahner *Theological Investigations* IV, London 1966, 309). '. . . le canon n'a jamais été

Now we are in a position to decide which of the two alternative statements offered just now is correct. The very idea of the church pre-existing the presence of Christ in her midst is theologically meaningless. The church is that community of people constituted as church by being personally 'addressed', called, by the living Christ. Christ is not 'able to be present' because we, 'the church', can fix things that way. We are the church because Christ is present to us, present in us, present as the objective significance of our gathering. We become 'more church' (which is to say that Christ becomes 'more present' to us) by responding, in word and deed, to his objective, constituting presence.

Once again there is an analogy to be made with ordinary human relationships. If A makes a declaration of love to B, B may, firstly, entirely fail to advert to A (in which case B is present so far as A is concerned, but A is not present so far as B is concerned); this is the situation between, the presence of Christ in his church and the unbeliever.[6] Secondly, B may advert to A with hostility (in which case they are mutually present, but in an unsatisfactory manner); this is the situation between the presence of Christ in his church and the believer who 'eats and drinks damnation to himself'. Thirdly, B

une profession de foi en la présence du Seigneur *comme telle* sous les espèces du pain et du vin, mais il a toujours été une profession de foi en la manière dont le sacrement agit dans la célébration, notamment comme source de la communion et de l'unité ecclesiale' (Manders, quoted in *Paroisse et Liturgie*, 1967, 255).

[6] I must leave on one side the question whether the (formal) unbeliever is, in many cases, an 'anonymous christian', and therefore whether the saving response of faith is often present in one who does not formally confess Christ.

may respond to A's presence with varying degrees of answering love and concern; this is the case when the presence of Christ in his church becomes 'fruitful' in the holiness of life in the Spirit. The objectivity of Christ's presence in the church is guaranteed by his promise: a promise to be personally with us, for us, concerned about us, relating to us, until the end of time. Persons become present to each other in the act of communicating with each other, and the sacramental system, in all its range and variety, is the language in which Christ keeps his promise.[7] The objectivity of Christ's presence in the church is not achieved or guaranteed either by 'mute bodiliness' or by the quality of our response.

Therefore we must say, both as a general theological truth, and in relation to the eucharistic assembly, that the presence of Christ pre-exists and is the essential precondition for the existence of the church and the celebration of her eucharist.[8]

So far, in spite of the fact that this is meant to be a discussion of 'whose sacrifice?' and of 'how' it is that the mass is a sacrifice, it might seem that the idea of sacrifice has not yet entered into the discussion. This is not in fact the case. The death and resurrection of Christ is the definitive, exhaustive statement of God's word in human flesh. The death and resurrection of Christ is the definitive form of God's disclosure to man of his effective care and concern for man. The death and resurrection of Christ is the definitive realisation of the presence of

[7] Cf ch 5.

[8] This is the truth defended by the doctrine that the church survives or the sacraments are celebrated *ex opere operato*, although most theologians today are agreed that a happier formulation would be *ex opere operantis Christi*.

God to man: Emmanuel.[9] One of the ways in which the death and resurrection of Christ can be described is by calling it a sacrifice, because it fulfils, completes, transcends, that class of human acts which, when we observe them in primitive or old testament religion, we call sacrifices.[10] It follows from this that, if that one definitive word of God to man which is the death and resurrection of Christ is to continue to be 'heard' in human history, men will thereby be 'hearing' the sacrifice of Christ. Christ will become present to them, and they to Christ, in that sacrifice-language which is the final statement of God to his people. Although there may be other terms than the term 'sacrifice' which we can use to describe the definitive statement of God's word in human flesh ('the paschal mystery', for example), it cannot be the case that Christ can become present to us (can speak to us, can personally address us) except in his death and resurrection, except as his death and resurrection, except as 'offering his sacrifice'.[11]

In view of the fact that the Letter to the Hebrews 'puts heavy stress on the unique nature of Christ's priest-

[9] On the death and resurrection of Christ as God's definitive word to man, cf *Constitution on Divine Revelation* 4.

[10] The death and resurrection of Christ is indeed a 'sacrifice for sin', because in that death and newness of life in God all alienation of man from God, and of brother from brother, is conquered and uprooted. But the originality, transcendence, and cosmic significance of that unique event is diminished by the tendency, observable in some protestant theology, to fit the cross into one pre-christian (old testament) category of religious acts: namely, the old testament 'sacrifice for sin' (cf E. M. B. Green, 'Christ's Sacrifice and Ours', *Guidelines* London 1967, 96, 99).

[11] This is, of course, a central theme of the letter to the Hebrews. For an excellent discussion of the letter in this context, cf F. X. Durrwell *The Resurrection* (London 1960) 136–46.

hood and sacrifice, emphasising the fact that it happened once for all time',[12] it should be clear that to say 'Christ continues to offer his sacrifice in the church', cannot mean that he continues to make his sacrifice. But neither can it mean that Christ, having finished his work, now does something else, called 'offering (pleading?) his completed sacrifice', for the death of Christ is his final deed, as it is, in the resurrection, the Father's final word.[13] To say that Christ 'continues to offer his sacrifice in the church' can only mean that the final word is heard, the final deed is (objectively) made present, in the life and celebration of God's faithful people.

The question that arises, therefore, is: how can this definitive speaking of the word which is the sacrifice of Christ, a speaking that took place two thousand years ago, continue to be heard today? The biblical answer is that 'the Spirit is sent', meaning that a community of men is constituted as 'hearers of the word', by the power of that word, which is the power, the life, the Spirit of God. In order to try to penetrate that answer a little more deeply there is, yet again, a useful analogy that can be drawn from ordinary human relationships.

A declaration of love is effective in the measure that it awakens a response of love on the part of the loved one. A declaration of love between two human beings

[12] Joseph Ratzinger, 'Is the Eucharist a Sacrifice?', in *Concilium* IV, 3 (1967) 35.

[13] '... the resurrection of Christ is not another event *after* his passion and death. In spite of the duration of time which intervenes, which is anyway an intrinsic component of even the most unified and indivisible act of spatio-temporal man, the resurrection is the manifestation of what happened in the death of Christ' (Karl Rahner, 'Dogmatic Questions on Easter', in *Theological Investigations* IV, London 1966, 128).

continues to be effective (and does not need to be re-peated) just for so long as the beloved can continue to trust that the original declaration holds good. If the answering love of the beloved weakens or dies, then the one who made the original declaration does not need to make another one—but only to draw the attention of the beloved to that original declaration's enduring validity; he has only to recall it for it to bear fruit again (unless, of course, the beloved has closed his heart, in which case the recalling is in vain). Now, although to recall the original declaration is, in one sense, to make it present again, it is not in any sense to make another declaration. Between two human beings, however, the original declaration of love can never be so total, so absolute and unconditional, that there is in fact no need to make a fresh declaration. In order that the beloved shall be continually assured of the declarer's love, it will be necessary to renew the declaration, to reinforce and repeat it; simply to recall it will be insufficient.

In the case of God's definitive declaration of love to man in the death and resurrection of Christ, there can be no question of the necessity, or even the possibility, of repeating this declaration, of making it again.[14] In

---

[14] Fr Schnackenburg's remarks about baptism are equally rele-vant to eucharistic doctrine: 'Because Christ died and rose as Representative and Substitute of redeemed mankind. . . . So soon as we establish through faith and baptism the union with him as our spiritual founder of the (new) race, we participate in that which happened to him. . . . The historical once for-all event that transpired on the cross stands immovable in its place and re-mains prior to that which we experience in baptism. Therefore we die "with Christ", it can never be the reverse, and on the basis of his resurrection we shall rise through him and in him and with him' (*Baptism in the Thought of St Paul* Oxford 1964, 114–15).

this unique case, the original declaration has the absolute, unconditional, eternal validity of God's eternal truth. Once God has spoken his word of love totally, there is nothing more to be said. The word of the Lord abides forever, and the process of speaking that word effectively in the hearts of men once awakened to hear it in the gift of the Spirit can only be a matter of recalling it, of calling it to mind. Such a calling to mind will be necessary, both because the word, which is to all men, has to be effectively heard by each man, and because, in the life of an individual or of a society, the answering love of man waxes and wanes, or even dies. Therefore we can say that, if Christ is to continue to be present (to speak) in human history in the unique act of his death and resurrection, then his presence can only be achieved by means of a recalling of the past event which is effective in the answering love and praise which it draws from the men to whom, and by whom, it is recalled.[15] In other words the sacrifice of Christ will continue to be present in history through its effective commemoration, which commemoration, as effective, draws from the men to whom God in Christ is thus made present in the Spirit the praise of faithful love and service.

The crucial question (at least for a Roman catholic) is: are the concepts of 'recall' and 'effectiveness' (in re-

[15] The reformation polemic obscured the identity (liturgically and theologically) of 'testimony' (God's word of reconciliation) and 'sacrifice' (our response); cf James F. McCue, 'Luther and Roman Catholicism on the Mass as Sacrifice', in *Journal of Ecumenical Studies* II (Duquesne 1965) 217. Our response of praise in the power of the Spirit, our 'eucharist', is God's word of reconciliation to us, achieved on Calvary, effectively commemorated in the celebration. (Cf, in addition to the previous chapter, Ratzinger, 39–40.)

conciliation, grace, forgiveness, brotherhood—the 'fruit' of Calvary) adequate to describe 'how' Christ in his sacrifice is present in our action, our 'eucharist'? It is my firm belief that the answer is 'yes'.[16] Those theologians who would claim that the objective reality of our eucharist as a participation in Christ's sacrifice demands a third concept (we recall his sacrifice, and receive the fruit of his sacrifice, and his sacrifice is objectively made present) seem to me to be making a category mistake. 'Objective presence' and 'presence in communication' (in sign, in disclosure of meaning) are only seen as two essentially distinct and contrasted modes of being if it is assumed that the correct model for all forms of presence (and so for personal, and sacramental presence) is the spatial juxtaposition of inanimate objects.[17] But while it is undoubtedly the case that, in the celebration of the sacraments, Christ is present in his bodiliness,[18] the fact that the mode of this presence is sacramental makes it necessary for us to reject such a model as seriously misleading. A similar category confusion underlies such questions as: 'is Christ in heaven or is he on the altar?', because heaven is not a place and Christ is not locally present on the altar. 'Heaven' (the glory of God as shared by man) is the state in which the lamb, standing as it were slain, continues to recall his sacrifice to his people. He is (objectively) present to the people to whom, in the gift of his Spirit, he continues to be God's word-in-

[16] I have already suggested (cf 62–3) that this is the point of view adopted by Aquinas and the Council of Trent.

[17] Cf above, 110, note 4, and the excursus to the following chapter. For a fine discussion of the two concepts of 'objectivity' which meet here in head-on collision, cf Bernard Lonergan sj *Insight* (London 1958) 245–67, 375–84.

[18] Cf ch 5.

sacrifice of enduring love. He is (objectively) present to the people as the food they share, because the terms of the language in which they recall and realise the presence of his sacrifice is the covenant-supper which he left them for this purpose.

In other words, the sacrifice of Christ is not made present and then effectively recalled.[19] The sacrifice of Christ is (objectively) present to this group of people in being effectively recalled. This is why the question 'is the eucharist the sacrifice of Christ or the sacrifice of the church?' is meaningless. To say 'church' is to say 'people to whom Christ in his mysteries is objectively present'. To say 'act of the church' is to say 'act of Christ': apart from Christ, men and women are not (theologically) 'church' at all. That action, therefore, by means of which the church, in the power of the Spirit, effectively recalls the sacrifice of Christ is truly to be described as a sacrifice because it is the effective commemoration of the death and resurrection of Christ, the one, final, eternally valid sacrifice.

One further point. A declaration of love calls for an answer of love; a declaration of love evokes a response of love. If the response evoked is of a different form from, is other than, answering love, then we have a 'no',

[19] This would seem to be Fr Clark's position: 'The English Reformers denied any real objective presence of Christ in or with the Eucharistic elements, a denial which removes the foundation of the Catholic concept of sacrifice; for if Christ is not objectively present in the sacrament he cannot be offered there' (159; cf 264, 520). On the other hand, Karl Rahner insists that: 'It is not because Christ is present that we offer him as our sacrifice and receive him in communion, but the other way round' (IV 309; cf this whole essay on 'The Presence of Christ in the Sacrament of the Lord's Supper').

5+

not a 'yes' to the declaration. In the case of the death and resurrection of Christ, the declaration takes the form of that total statement of desired and achieved communion in life and love which is the consummation of sacrifice. Therefore the acceptance of the declaration, the answering 'yes' of man to God in the power of the Spirit, is of the same form as the declaration itself. In other words, if we cannot call the acceptance of the 'sacrifice-word' itself a sacrifice, then we have answered with a different word—with 'no' rather than 'yes'. Therefore although, as we have seen, the sacrificial nature of the eucharist depends upon its being the effective recalling of the cross of Christ (*quae fuit verum sacrificium*, as Aquinas said), nevertheless not only is it the case that the answering action of praise and love by which we accept the sacrificial word in our recalling of it must be termed sacrificial, but also it is hardly surprising that the language which Christ left us as the language of effective recall (the covenant-supper of the brotherhood) should be a language, a complex of words and gestures. which is recognisable, on its own terms, as sacrificial.

The answer, then, to the question 'whose sacrifice?' is: Christ's sacrifice made present in our sacrifice of praise, our 'eucharist'. The answer to the question 'how' is the mass a sacrifice depends upon a prior distinction. If the question means: how can we be sure that our human action is the effective recalling of Christ's sacrifice, then the answer is: because he promised to be with us all days, and we, in whom the response of faith has been awakened, are acting in obedience to his command. If the question means 'in what form is his sacrifice effectively commemorated?' then the answer is an empirical description of our action: a *sacrificium laudis*, a 'eucharist', in which bread is taken, broken, and shared, and the significance of this action is declared in our prayer of responding praise and thanksgiving for the *mirabilia Dei* and, centrally, for that definitive *mirabile* which is the sacrifice-word of Christ's death and resurrection.

If the previous chapter is read in the light of that rather rapid and schematic summary then it may, I hope, be granted that we have a theory of the mass which satisfactorily interprets the liturgical data. It may not be so obvious, however, that this theory satisfies the demands made upon the catholic theologian by the teaching of the Council of Trent. The point was made in the previous chapter that, although the relevant decree of Trent achieved an admirable theological balance, the dominant image of sacrifice that underlay the controversies of the period was that of pre-christian forms of sacrifice,[20] and we would expect this fact to emerge, from time to time, in the council's choice of terms.

[20] Perhaps this point has been sufficiently stressed in the previous chapter. But it is so important that the following reminder may be helpful: 'Catholic theologians in modern times have taken great pains, quite uselessly, to prove to Protestants that the Eucharist is *also* a sacrifice, *even though* it is obviously a meal. Because of this, liturgists of the Baroque Age were compelled to dissimulate, to diminish as far as possible this aspect of a meal in order to ratify their own concept of sacrifice, which was that of their adversaries as well....In antiquity the Eucharist was seen as the sacrifice of the Christians *because* it was the sacred meal of the Christian community. The texts of the Fathers are so clear and consistent on this point that it can only be denied by a kind of wilful blindness' (L. Bouyer *Rite and Man* London 1963, 82–3).

The teaching of Trent on the sacrifice of the mass may be summarised in the following six points:[21]

1. The mass is a visible sacrifice.

2. The mass makes present the sacrifice of the cross, and serves for all time as a memorial thereof.

3. In the mass the salutary power of Calvary is applied for the remission of our sins.

4. The mass is a propitiatory sacrifice because in it Christ is contained and offered.

5. The mass is rightly offered for both the living and the dead.

6. The mass in no way takes away from Calvary.

Let us take each of these six points in turn.

1. In the first place, it is fairly obvious that the celebration of the eucharist by a group of people is a visible affair. The sacrifice of Christ is not recalled simply by mental acts on someone's part, but by people gathering together and saying and doing certain things.

In the second place, I have suggested how it is that this visible thing which is the celebration of the eucharist can, and should, be called a sacrifice. It is, of course, true that our (visible) *sacrificium laudis* is only recognisable as the presence, in effective recall, of Christ's sacrifice, to faith.

2. This second point would seem to be a summary of all that I have tried to say in the foregoing pages. And to say that, in the eucharist, the sacrifice of Christ is only present to faith, is not to deny the objectivity of that presence, but simply to say that the death and resurrection of Christ is only God's word of salvation to him who believes.

[21] I have taken this summary from McCue, 224.

3. In other words, the eucharist is not simply the re-calling of God's word-in-sacrifice on Calvary (*nuda com-memoratio*), but is the effective recalling of that word of love. The remission of sins is, precisely, the answer-ing love, faith, commitment of man to God in the power of the Spirit which is awakened, reawakened, deepened, in the effective hearing of the word.

4. It is in this, and the following point, that the 'domi-nant image' problem arises most acutely. If the mass is in any sense a sacrifice, if it is the sacrifice of Christ made present in our sacrifice of praise, if the verb 'to offer' is the verb employed in conjunction with the noun 'sacrifice', then it must be logically correct to say that, in the mass, Christ is offered. It may also be the case that this particular formulation of the meaning of our action is misleading, and open to serious misunderstanding if it is not handled very carefully, but that is another matter.

'In what sense is the mass a propitiatory sacrifice? First of all it must be stated very plainly that the Mass is not propitiatory in the sense that it somehow wins over a hostile God ... the Mass is propitiatory in that it effects—as Luther and Trent[22] both insist—the for-giveness of sins of those who participate by faith.'[23] Once

[22] '... docet sancta Synodus, sacrificium istud vere propitia-torium esse, per ipsumque fieri, ut, si cum vero corde et recta fide, cum metu ac reverentia, contriti ac poenitentes ad Deum accedamus, misericordiam consequamur et gratiam inveniamus in auxilio opportuno (Heb 4.16)' (Denzinger 940).

[23] McCue, 227–8. 'The sacrifice of the Mass creates no new and saving will in God vis-à-vis the world, which did not already exist through the Cross (and only through the Cross!) ... the gracious will of God, founded exclusively in the reconciliation of the Cross, becomes visible in the sacrifice of the mass and

again, the fact that this use of language may be open to serious misunderstanding is another matter.

5. Christ died for all men. The definitive word of God in human flesh is addressed to all mankind. Therefore the eucharist, as the language of recall, addresses us with and expresses the same universality as the cross itself. In the eucharist we 'hear' the declaration of God's love made, not merely to ourselves, the handful gathered in this room, but to all mankind. If, therefore, our acceptance of God's word (for the language of recall is the language of answering praise and love) is the expression of a narrower concern than that manifested by the word himself, then it is a 'no' and not a 'yes' to that word. Our response is only authentic insofar as it expresses our universal concern. If, in the celebration of the eucharist, the 'little flock' is not conscious of being the representative community, if the mass is not 'offered for both the living and the dead' (for all the living and the dead, though it is entirely proper that, on any given occasion, our prayer and concern may focus on some particular human need),[24] then we are making a mockery of the love of God.

6. It should be clear that this final point from the teaching of the Council of Trent is central to all that I have tried to say about the relationship of the eucharist to that definitive moment in human history which is the death of Christ on Calvary.

---

comes to man in his concrete situation' (Karl Rahner, 'Die velen Messen und das eine Opfer', in *Zeitschrift für katholische Theologie* 71, 1949, quoted by McCue, 227–8).

[24] In saying this, I am taking it for granted (discussion of the point lies outside the scope of this chapter) that 'praying for the dead' is an entirely proper christian activity.

It would seem to be the case that the approach to the theology of the eucharist which I have adopted in these chapters might well prove acceptable, at least as a basis for discussion, to many christians outside the Roman communion.[25] This is not to suggest, of course, that our problems are at an end. While all of us, I suppose, would agree that a common search of the scriptures is the proper context for ecumenical discussion, none of us can be sure that we are 'hearing' the scriptural word without distortion so long as we continue to 'hear' it so differently. Roman catholics are often accused of reading the bible in the light of their own dogmatic presuppositions. But I am bound to ask, for example, whether evangelical understanding of the sacrificial nature of the death of Christ does not sometimes owe more to Luther's theological perspectives than to contemporary exegesis of pauline and johannine theology.[26] Be that as it may, it can hardly be denied that there is a considerable convergence in eucharistic doctrine and practice. But is such agreement as exists illusory? Has it been won at too great a price? Mr McCue, in his

[25] Cf Wim Boelens sj 'Eucharistic Developments in the Evangelical Church' *Concilium* IV, 3 (1967) 48–56; a brilliant summary of the present state of the question written from a Roman catholic viewpoint.

[26] It seems to be the case that, for both Fr Clark and Mr Green, the 'dominant image' of sacrifice which underlies their treatment is that of old testament ritual sacrifice (in other words, they both tend to discuss the question from within the sixteenth-century problematic), and that, as a result, they tend to give insufficient weight to the unity of the paschal mystery (cf Clark, 284–6; Green, 98–106; amongst recent exegetical studies of the new testament data, cf David Stanley sj *Christ's Resurrection in Pauline Soteriology, Analecta Biblica 13* Rome 1961).

article to which I have so often referred, follows the statement of his thesis[27] by the honest admission that, to many people, he may seem to have set himself an impossible task: 'It would seem, therefore, that all that can be done in considering "Luther and Roman Catholicism on the Mass as Sacrifice", would be to catalogue the differences and perhaps to show how these are rooted in more fundamental theological options'.[28]

This is, of course, precisely the position adopted by Fr Francis Clark SJ in his book *Eucharistic Sacrifice and the Reformation*, a book which, thanks to the author's massive erudition, has quickly become a standard work on the subject. It is, however, possible that Fr Clark's regretfully negative judgement on the proximity of adequate ecumenical agreement on this central issue is unduly affected by his methodological presuppositions. It is insufficient, in order to demonstrate that the reformers rejected the word of God in Christ, to show that the common teaching of catholic theologians of the period was orthodox (in the sense that it was logically consistent with propositions affirmed as of faith by the magisterium), and that the reformers rejected this teaching. The relationship between the 'deposit of faith' and 'the manner in which it is presented' is not quite so simple.

In writing his book, Fr Clark was convinced, surely correctly, that no true service was being done to the ecumenical movement by the survival of the myth that late-medieval eucharistic theology was corrupt and un-

[27] 'It will be the thesis of the present paper that there is a substantial identity of view between Luther and Roman Catholicism on the understanding of the Mass as sacrifice' (McCue, 206).
[28] McCue, 207.

orthodox, at least at the popular level, and that the sharpness of the reformers' protest could be explained as a rejection, not of truly catholic doctrine, but of this corrupt popular theology. Accordingly, he set himself the task of bringing his considerable learning to bear on the problem, and believes that he has demonstrated that late-medieval theology was, in the matter of the mass, not only orthodox but stolidly conservative. As one who is not an historian, I am not competent to judge Fr Clark's book from the point of view of historical scholarship. I can only say that, within his chosen limits, he has established a very formidable case which it would seem impossible for future scholars to ignore. He has therefore made an important contribution to the history of eucharistic doctrine, and has placed the rest of us very considerably in his debt. But is this the end of the matter?

A proposition may be considered orthodox if, when employed with a certain linguistic convention, or frame of reference, it neither contradicts nor significantly departs from those judgements, formulated from the same viewpoint and generally accepted (either as a result of solid theological consensus, or as a result of their employment in a weighty pronouncement of the magisterium) as being representative of catholic belief on the topic in question. To say, however, that a proposition, or set of propositions, is orthodox according to such criteria is to say something whose importance, however genuine, is limited. The truth-value of propositions is not to be ascertained simply in the abstract, in isolation from their use and employment in human affairs. If what the church is doing, in the concrete, can reason-

5*

ably be said to be significantly different from what she ought to be doing, then the theory according to which she interprets her activity may be calculated to mislead, even if that same theory, when employed as the interpretation of a more adequate state of concrete activity, were irreproachable.

It can hardly be denied that what the church was doing (and she teaches as much by what she does as by what she says) in the late medieval period was calculated to give the impression that the mass was something 'done' by the celebrant and 'watched' by the church at large. The impression was further given that the hearing by the church of the proclamation of Christ's saving mysteries, and the sharing together in the brotherhood of eucharistic communion, were not central to what it meant to 'offer the mass' (because, in fact, the church at large did not hear the saving word and did not, as a matter of regular practice, share the meal of covenant-sacrifice). Therefore the question must be asked: however orthodox the theory according to which the action was interpreted, is it not inevitable that this theory should have been 'heard', in the concrete, by preacher and people, as a somewhat less than adequate statement of the meaning of the mass?[29]

[29] 'When theologians who defend the sacrificial concept of the Mass seem not to be disturbed by the development of a sub-Christian understanding of sacrifice within Roman Catholic piety, then there is at least some justification for thinking that the piety does express the doctrine. It is a very natural assumption, though in a surprising number of cases it turns out to be false, that practice and doctrine will agree, and that the meaning of the latter is best understood by means of the former.... Among Roman Catholics, the liturgical movement has taken seriously the responsibility of making practice express doctrine' (McCue, 233).

In other words, it is possible to criticise Fr Clark's book, and that theological method which it represents, on the grounds that it shows a markedly non-historical attitude towards conceptual truth, and a failure to take with sufficient seriousness the relationship between theology and christian living. So, for example, having listed the practical abuses that were prevalent in the late-medieval period, Fr Clark says:

All this illustrates the pressing need for reform in the late medieval Church (a need that could have been met, and in the Counter-Reformation was met,[30] without jettisoning the essentials of Catholic faith), but *it cannot be of decisive significance in the present enquiry.*[31]

The reformation debate was unsatisfactory both because neither side appreciated the methodological gulf that divided them, and because the demands of polemic inevitably resulted in doctrinal imbalance. The tendencies latent in the positions adopted by the contestants have been well described by Dr Mascall:

What in fact is offered in the Eucharist, and who is doing the offering? Late medieval Catholicism had a quite simple answer: the priest is offering Christ. The Reformers had a quite simple answer too: the worshippers are offering, first their praise and then themselves. It is not Christ that is being offered; he offered himself once for all upon the Cross; all that we can do

---

[30] In view of the fact that he rightly lists, amongst the areas that needed reforming, the lack of active participation in the mass and, in particular, the infrequency of communion, this is a surprising assertion.

[31] Clark, 63–4 (my stress).

is to remember his offering with gratitude and then offer ourselves. Now what has happened with both these answers is that the unity of Christ with his Church has simply fallen to pieces.[32]

In other words, any theology of the eucharist which maintains that the question 'whose sacrifice?' and the 'how' question can be adequately answered either in terms of 'the sacrifice of Christ' or of 'the sacrifice of the church' has got into such considerable confusion in its understanding of the relationship of Christ to his church that clarity and intelligibility can hardly be hoped for, and a departure from christian orthodoxy is, although not inevitable, at least an ever-present danger.[33] Fr Clark rejects Dr Mascall's analysis because, as he points out,[34] there is ample evidence that the catholic theologians of the period clearly understood that 'the church's priestly function derives from and is wholly dependent on the priesthood of Christ'. But is this alone sufficient to en-

---

[32] *The Recovery of Unity* (London 1958) 140–1, quoted by Clark, 325.

[33] 'His atoning sacrifice is the *root* of our salvation; our responsive sacrifice of praise, thanksgiving, and self-dedication is the *fruit* of it' (Green, 117). I can imagine no theologian, of any denomination, who would quarrel with that excellent statement. But if the 'fruit' is not to be a 'merely human work' it must also be the praise and self-dedication of Christ acting, in his Spirit, in his unworthy members ('a branch cannot bear fruit all by itself, but must remain part of the vine', Jn 15.4). In this sense (and not in any sense that would derogate from the completeness of the historical act of the glorifying cross, the source of the Spirit) is our sacrifice a sharing in the sacrifice of Christ. The patristic formula: 'the whole Christ offers the whole Christ' does not have, in the minds of those who employ it, the sinister implications which Mr Green suspects (cf 111).

[34] Cf Clark, 335–8.

sure that, in speaking of 'the church offering', or of 'Christ now offering', one is speaking of one and the same thing: namely, the praise and worship of a community whose words and gestures are both the language in which God's word-in-sacrifice of the cross is presented and their acceptance of this word? I think not, and it seems that, as a result, Fr Clark too readily identifies the (orthodox if misleading) language and method of one school of catholic theology with 'catholic theology', *tout court*.

This is suggested by the very first page of his book:

> The belief that Jesus Christ is daily offered on the Church's altar for the welfare of the living and the dead, his body and blood really present under the appearances of bread and wine, the belief that he has instituted a priestly order of men sharing in his own sacerdotal power and authority through whom he continues to offer his propitiatory sacrifice to the eternal Father, in order to apply to mankind in every age and place the benefits of redemption and salvation won for them by his death on the Cross—this is for Catholics one of the fundamentals of their faith.[35]

But in such a formulation of certain aspects of catholic belief, a formulation which so uncompromisingly interprets an image other than the concrete image of the worshipping community in the sign of the covenant-supper, a formulation which so resolutely omits all reference to such equally basic concepts as the priestly church, the praise and faith of the worshipping people, the fraternal communion for which the mass was insti-

[35] Clark, 3.

tuted,[36] the commemorative nature of the celebration—
is it not the case that, since these concepts also are necessary for arriving at the catholic meaning of the mass, a
certain imbalance has been introduced right from the
beginning?

At the end of the book there occurs another passage
which serves to confirm this suspicion:

> Who or what is offered in the Eucharistic sacrifice?
> The answer of Catholic theology is, first and above
> all, Christ himself. The Eucharist is a truly availing
> sacrifice because therein the everlasting victim of Cal-
> vary is objectively present and is offered in order to
> perpetuate his saving work through all time. At the
> other extreme is the answer of the majority of Angli-
> can churchmen from the sixteenth century onwards,
> which was that of Cranmer and his fellow Reformers.
> In an applied sense the Eucharist, like all the prayers
> and actions of Christians, may be called a sacrifice. In
> it may be offered our lauds and thanks, our prayers
> and alms, even ourselves, our souls and bodies—but
> not Christ.[37]

If that summary were an adequate statement of catholic
and anglican belief, we should be forced to conclude
that Dr Mascall's analysis was valid even for today, and
that the 'unity of Christ with his Church has simply
fallen to pieces'. A number of recent and authoritative
statements suggest, however, that the picture is not quite
so dark:

> In the Holy Eucharist or Lord's Supper, constantly
> repeated and always including both word and sacra-

---

[36] Cf Trent: 'ut sumerent, tradidit' (Denzinger 938).
[37] Clark, 516.

ment, we proclaim and celebrate a memorial of the saving acts of God (1 Cor 11.23–6). What God did in the incarnation, life, death, resurrection and ascension of Christ, he does not do again. The events are unique; they cannot be repeated or extended or continued. Yet in this memorial we do not only recall past events: God makes them present through the Holy Spirit who takes the things of Christ and declares them to us, thus making us participants in Christ (1 Cor 1.9). Despite many disagreements regarding Holy Communion and despite the desire of many for a fuller statement, we are drawn at least to agree that the Lord's supper, a gift of God to his Church, is a sacrament of the presence of the crucified and glorified Christ until he come, and a means whereby the sacrifice of the cross, which we proclaim, is operative within the Church. In the Lord's Supper the members of the body of Christ are sustained in their unity with their Head and Saviour who offered himself on the cross: by him, with him and in him who is our great High Priest and Intercessor we offer to the Father, in the power of the Holy Spirit, our praise, thanksgiving and intercession. With contrite hearts we offer ourselves as a living and holy sacrifice, a sacrifice which must be expressed in the whole of our daily lives. Thus united to our Lord, and to the Church triumphant, and in fellowship with the whole Church on earth, we are renewed in the covenant sealed by the blood of Christ. In the Supper we also anticipate the marriage-supper of the Lamb in the Kingdom of God.[38]

[38] P. C. Rodger and L. Vischer (eds) *The Fourth World Con-*

Christ's sacrificial work on the Cross was *for* us; he died as our Redeemer. He who once died and is now alive for ever more is also *in* us; he dwells in our hearts by faith. And in virtue of this union, we are now identified with him both in his death and passion, and in his resurrection, life and glory. There is but one Body, of which he is the Head and we are the members; and we are made one with each other because we are one in him. In our baptism we were united with him by the likeness of his death (Rom 6.5) and in the Eucharist we abide in him as we eat his Body and drink his Blood (Jn 6.56). So we come to the Father in and through Jesus our great High Priest. We have nothing to offer that we have not first received, but we offer our praise and thanksgiving for Christ's sacrifice for us and so present it again, and ourselves in him, before the Father. We are partakers of the sacrifice of Christ (1 Cor 10.16), and this is shown forth by our sacrifice of praise to God continually through Christ (Heb 13.15), and by our life of service and suffering for his sake in the world (Phil 3.9–10). We ourselves, incorporate in the mystical body of Christ, are the sacrifices we offer. Christ with us offers us in himself to God.[39]

It could possibly be objected that, although that statement indicates a remarkable consensus in the matter of eucharistic doctrine, such a verbal consensus does not represent anything more than a deliberately ambiguous

---

ference on *Faith and Order, Montreal 1963* (London 1964) 73–4 (articles 116 and 117 of the section reports).

[39] *Report of the Lambeth Conference 1958* II, 84, quoted by Clark, 519. Cf also the *Constitution on the Liturgy* 6, 7, 47, 48.

attempt to paper over the cracks because, beneath this 'merely verbal' agreement different people 'really' hold different and often incompatible doctrinal positions.[40]

The first thing to be said about this objection is that any set of words is capable of more than one interpretation. To secure agreement 'beyond' one formula, another interpretative formula would be required, and so on *ad infinitum*.

The second thing to be said is that, because human beings communicate by means of language, any agreement between people will be a verbal agreement and, since language discloses meaning, it is difficult to see what is meant by a 'merely' verbal agreement, when that agreement has in fact been reached between real people who may be presumed to have understood each other's meaning.[41]

[40] This seems to be the objection of Fr Clark (516–22) and Mr Green. 'The very word "partakers" admits of three interpretations, two of which do not apply to the Church's offering. Thus we do not partake in Christ's sacrifice as *offerers*. He offered it without our aid and on our behalf. We are not partakers in that sacrifice as *victims*. He alone was the victim, dying in lonely isolation in our stead. But we are indeed partakers in that sacrifice as *beneficiaries*' (Green, 110). I would agree that the first two interpretations do not apply to the church's offering if they are understood as in any way 'taking away from Calvary'. But in view of the fact that no catholic would wish them to be understood in this sense, perhaps the Lambeth formula is not so bad after all!

[41] 'An agreement about truth always takes place between human beings in a sociological milieu, and when it is attained *there*, it is, none the less, attained. But it is attained there when it is attained in words and propositions (ie *verbally*, if you like) as used by men who pay attention to what they hear and think about what they say. There is a danger that, particularly in controversial theology, a neurotic fear that we are perhaps not

It is further to be noticed that the degree of agreement or disagreement can be tested, for example, by an examination of the forms of worship employed by the various parties. If one party is worshipping in a way which seems to indicate that he understands the doctrinal formula, by which he interprets his action, in a manner which is radically different from that of his partner in the dialogue, then certainly a further mutual examination of the meaning of the formula would be entirely in order.

Finally, no one theology in the catholic church has the right to claim that it is the sole 'catholic' interpretative theory for conciliar pronouncements and liturgical practice. If there exist within the catholic church (as there undoubtedly do) a variety of theological interpretations of eucharistic belief, each of which is recognised by the members of the church as orthodox; if it is also the case that one or other of these theologies is virtually identical with an equally 'respectable' theology em-

---

"really", not "in our furthest depths" at one, may destroy such unity as might exist. . . . In order to have the right to live in separate Churches, we should have to be certain (to put it in broad general terms) that we were unmistakably disunited about the truth, and not merely be slightly uncertain whether we were really entirely at one. . . . We should not, then, say at once of every formula of agreement: Oh, yes, but go a little deeper into it and discrepancies will soon appear; the general terms in which it is stated are simply hiding them! As though we could not have the very same suspicion about all the unity within the Catholic Church!' (Karl Rahner SJ 'Zur Theologie der Gnade. Bemerkungen zu dem Buche von Hans Küng: Rechtfertigung. Die Lehre Karl Barths und eine katholische Besinnung', in *Tübinger Theologische Quartalschrift* CXXXVIII, 1958, 40–77; quoted in Hans Küng, *The Council and Reunion* London 1961, 174–7).

ployed in another denomination, then it can no longer be said with absolute certainty that there exists between the two churches a difference in faith.

Certainly nobody would pretend that christians of all denominations are yet reconciled in the matter of eucharistic doctrine. Certainly the word of God is not served by vague and misguided attempts to gloss over doctrinal differences. But, in view of the fact that the gulf which separates any two catholic theologians often seems currently to be as wide as that which separates the catholic from his anglican or protestant brother (as wide but, as I suggested just now, not apparently wider); in view of the fact that the catholics do not find their differences in theology sufficient cause to break off the sacramental communion which binds them in Christ, must we not ask whether, in ecumenical encounter, there is not often present the silent assumption that 'of course we are divided in faith', when perhaps this has ceased, under the healing grace of God, to be the case? But to ask such a question is to raise issues which go far beyond the limited concerns of this chapter.

5
The eucharist: sacrament of Christ's presence in the world

It is impossible to say everything at once. There is only one word in which everything can be expressed at once, and it is the word of God. It is therefore necessary for the theologian, or for anybody else who is trying to grapple with the problem of human existence, to divide in order to conquer. He must concentrate on one thing at a time. The danger, however, is that by devoting all his energies to fighting a skirmish in one small corner of the battlefield, the theologian will lose sight of the significance which this skirmish has, or should have, in the campaign as a whole. The expert tactician is always a bad strategist. In his recent book, Dom Sebastian Moore has made the point very well:

> It is only the attempt to answer *this* question (What the hell does it all *mean*?), put wholly and honestly to oneself and with a preparedness to hear answers from unexpected quarters, that can issue in a real theology. Paradoxically, the shirking of this task is more of a danger today than ever before. For not only

does the far greater amount of learning required ex-
acerbate the factor of exhaustion. In addition to this,
within the privileged circle of professional theology
an original and adventurous mind will, through the
modern theological disciplines, arrive at very radical
shifts of perspective and involve the theologian in
violent clashes with his conservative peers, so that he
easily comes to think that by these shifts and in these
consequent clashes he is being 'contemporary'. He
will easily fail to realize that what is *within the circle*
a revolution appears to the wider world (that is wait-
ing to hear from him) to be a purely domestic battle,
offering no more than the journalistic interest of a
palace revolution.[1]

Now, although I do not flatter myself that I have either
an original or adventurous mind, it is at least fairly
clear that the discussion of the eucharist in the three
previous chapters has been carried on 'within the circle'.
In this chapter, therefore, I want to take one aspect of
the theology of the eucharist and try to show how a shift
in our understanding of this leads to a corresponding
shift in our understanding of the society in which we
live. The aspect I have chosen concerns the *presence* of
Christ in the world.

The presence of Christ in the eucharist

We must begin by being quite clear about one thing.
If Christ is simply absent from human history since
Easter day, then there is no such thing as christianity.
There are people for whom Jesus of Nazareth is simply
an historical memory. Such people may acknowledge his

[1] Sebastian Moore *God is a New Language* (London 1967) 83.

nobility of character, respect the force of his ethical teaching: but they are not christians. It is clear from the new testament that what constituted the primitive church was the consciousness of this community that it only existed, as a community, in the presence of the Spirit of the risen Christ. To put the point another way: to tell people, on the basis of the new testament, how they ought to live, does not constitute the preaching of the gospel, the good news, of Jesus Christ. To announce to a society that its attitudes and structures are negative and inhuman, and to tell it that things ought to be otherwise, is hardly good news. It is a depressing statement of what most people are dimly aware of anyway. The witness of christianity is only the announcement of good news if its primary statement concerns the here-and-now availability of the resources with which to revolutionise human society in the love of God. The witness of christianity, in other words, is only the preaching of the gospel if it announces the fact and the presence of the risen Christ.

Article 7 of the *Constitution on the Liturgy* is a magnificent statement of the forms of the presence of the risen Christ in the worshipping assembly:

To accomplish so great a work, Christ is always present in his Church, especially in her liturgical actions. He is present in the sacrifice of the Mass, not only in the person of his minister . . . but especially under the eucharistic species. By his power he is present in the sacraments, so that when a man baptises, it is really Christ himself who baptises. He is present in his Word, since it is he himself who speaks when the holy scriptures are read in the Church. He is present, lastly, when the Church prays and sings, for he promised: 'Where two or three are gathered together in my name, there am I in the midst of them' (Mt 18.20).

1 *In the gathered community*

That article mentions a number of ways in which Christ is present in his church. I want to concentrate on three of them: his presence in the gathered community, his presence in the word, his presence in the food. I think that there can be little doubt but that, if one asked many catholics 'in what way is Christ really present in the church?' the immediate answer would be 'in the blessed sacrament'. But the immediacy and ease of that reply shows a distortion in our christian thinking. Here I have to pick my words with care, because, in current theological debate, to suggest that our understanding of the presence of Christ in the blessed sacrament is not correctly situated in terms of our wider understanding of the christian mystery is to touch a sensitive nerve, and to invite misunderstanding. It will, I hope, become clear that I am not denying that the risen Christ is really, truly, and substantially present under the forms of bread and wine. What I said was, that if the question 'in what way is Christ really present in the Church?' draws the immediate and easy reply 'in the blessed sacrament', then we have shown up a distortion in our christian thinking.

To substantiate this charge, let me remind you of a line of thought that is commonly found in popular presentations, written and oral, of catholic doctrine. Here is a quotation from a CTS pamphlet last printed in 1962: 'Thus it is that a Catholic church is seldom empty. It is always a home with one permanent resident, and he is the Sovereign Lord of all. This should not be surprising; after all, God in the Old Testament was with his people in the cloud and the pillar of fire; is it not to be expected that he would be present in an even better way in the New Testament?'[2] Let us follow the author's invitation and turn to the new testament. Certainly the apostolic church was convinced that the Lord of history, whose guiding and saving presence to his people was symbolised, in the exodus, in the cloud and pillar of fire, was present in an even better way to his new people. But the most casual reading of the new testament makes it clear that what they had in mind was his presence, in the Spirit, in the hearts and minds of the christian community.

The message of the new testament is about people, about humanity renewed, reborn to freedom and the love of God, through water and the Holy Spirit. In other words, the immediate and primary answer to the question 'in what way is Christ really present in the church?' must be 'in *us*'. This is not to deny that there may be other modes of Christ's presence in the world; it is to affirm that whatever other modes of presence there may be are for the sake of his presence in his people.

To imply, as the kind of popular theology to which I referred does, that apart from that particular presence of Christ which is his presence in the consecrated bread and wine, he is absent from this city or this town is to

[2] E. R. Hull *What the Catholic Church is and What she Teaches* (London 1962) 27.

deny, by implication, the very heart of the christian message. The 'even better way' of Christ's presence in the new testament refers primarily to his presence in the people who live, now not they, but Christ lives in them.

The first stage, then, is to acknowledge that the fundamental presence in the world of the risen Christ is his presence in people. But the second stage is to realise that his presence is not first achieved in individuals, who then happen to come together to acknowledge the fact. It may be true that some groups of human beings are structured in this way: free associations of individuals who decide to meet to further some common interest. But the church as she exists in the concrete, the eucharistic assembly, is not that sort of get-together.

Sin separates; it separates men from each other and from God; it fractures human community, warping individuals into isolated pockets of mutual fear, ignorance, and antagonism. Love, the redemptive love of God, unites; it unites men with each other and with God; it creates human community, opening individuals out into fully developed personal relationships of mutual trust, knowledge, and love. The work of our redemption is the work of building human community. It is the work of God, and therefore, in Christ, renewed human community pre-exists the recognition and acceptance of it by the individual. We are called to renewed community by God, through Christ, in the Spirit. Our coming together as the community of believers is the expression of our acceptance of this call; our recognition of the situation in which, by faith, we find ourselves: a situation of community in the love of God.

Now you see why it is that the *Constitution*, when it

refers to that fundamental presence of Christ in the world which is his presence in people, does not say that he is present in 393 individuals, who meet together to compare notes about it. It says, quoting Matthew: 'Where two or three are gathered together in my name (by my power), there am I in the midst of them'.

2 *In the word proclaimed*

Men are brought to recognise, and to become involved in, the structure of salvation, as the construction of renewed human community, by faith. And faith is the response of the individual to the personal message of God's redeeming love. One person can only respond, in trust and love, to the message of another, if that other is making his appeal, his declaration of love, here and now. If I read in a novel that John said to Bertha: 'I love you', I may say 'good for Bertha', but the declaration of love does not affect, does not implicate, me. If I read in the paper that some great and good man has said: 'All men are my brothers; I love all men', I may appreciate his solicitude, but I may still not feel myself personally involved in this declaration of love. The only way in which I can be unavoidably implicated in a declaration of love, forced either to accept or reject it, is if the other person, here and now, makes that declaration to me. In other words faith, as a personal commitment to the risen Christ, is only possible if, in the proclamation of the gospel, Christ is really present.

Because the gospel the church has to proclaim concerns the announcement of the fact and possibility of renewed human community in the love of God, 'the teaching of the church' is, basically, the church herself, as the sign and the beginning of this renewed community. The verbal proclamation of the message is merely the articulation of the community's self-consciousness, of the community's reality. The initial statement of this self-consciousness, which remains normative for all future generations, is the scriptures. The scriptures remain normative because they are the articulation of faith by that initial community which received the fullness of the word made flesh, full of grace and truth. But this written word is not a dead word. Christ continues to be present in the message, as the message, in the proclamation of that message throughout history. Because the verbal message was born of the community, as that community's self-expression, because it is the continual call to community, therefore the fullest realisation of Christ's real presence as word, as declaration of love, is the proclamation of the scriptures (which includes the preaching and, above all, the *anaphora*) in the context of the eucharistic assembly. This is why the *Constitution* says: 'He is present in his word, since it is he himself who speaks when the holy scriptures are read in the Church'.

3 *In the food shared*

I hope it will be agreed that if most catholics were really alive to the two forms of Christ's real presence in the eucharistic assembly that I have mentioned so far, his presence in the community and his presence in the word, then their understanding of that activity known as 'going to mass' would already have been profoundly transformed and deepened. And it is this sort of transformation of people and their attitudes that the phrase 'liturgical reform' primarily refers to; not changes from Latin to English, or from six candles to two.

If a group of people are gathered for a specific purpose, the purpose of their gathering can be declared in several ways. The most obvious way would be for one of them to say what they were doing: 'Ladies and gentlemen, we are here this evening. . . .' But they could declare the purpose of their meeting by gestures, without using words. One person meets another who has just undergone some great sadness or disappointment: a squeeze of the hand, a facial expression, could perhaps say more than words could; the gesture would be a sort of language. A Romeo meets his Juliet for a brief second (neither of them have time to stop); he gives her a box of whatever chocolates the television advertisers currently decide are suitable for the purpose. The gift of the chocolates says something: it is a form of language.

In the ordinary way, we use a combination of words and gestures with which to declare our meaning. This is the way in which the sacraments operate. In the case of the sacraments, however, we do not decide what words and gestures shall be the language of our christian encounter. The language has already, in its essentials, been given to us by Christ. This is necessary, since our purpose in coming together is not simply to encounter each other, but to encounter each other in Christ. We can only be sure that our encounter is an encounter in Christ, an encounter with Christ, if the language we employ, the words and gestures we use, is the language we have been given by Christ for this purpose. To preserve the objective reality of our sacramental assemblies, to prevent them from being the ineffectual expression of our subjective attitudes and desires, it is necessary that we do the things he told us to do in memory of him.

When we gather, then, to celebrate the eucharist, the preordained language is that complex of words and gestures that goes to make up the last supper, the supper of covenant sacrifice, in the celebration of which we are, here and now, incorporated into the paschal mystery through our incorporation into the person of the risen Christ. Notice that word 'incorporation'. To be embodied in Christ, to become more fully the body of Christ, is the very meaning of the church. I made this point earlier when I said that the meaning of the church was renewed human community in the Spirit of the risen Christ.

We are gathered because we are the body of Christ. We gather to become more fully the body of Christ. Therefore the meaning of the language we employ to declare what we are doing, must be the body of Christ. Language is a means of communication; the purpose of our gathering, which we declare and achieve in word and gesture, is communion in the body of Christ.

What are the terms of the language we employ in the eucharist? They are, apart from the words of the canon of the mass, bread broken and shared, the language of a fraternal meal, a common expression of human community. Therefore any unbeliever, who happens to drop in to mass, should be able to realise that what we have here is a fraternity, expressing their brotherhood through sharing in a fraternal meal. If he further listens to the words of the canon, specifying this general gesture, he will realise that this fraternal meal is closely linked to the death and resurrection of somebody called the Son of God. But only the gift of faith enables a man to say, as he points to the assembled group of people: 'this is the body of Christ; what makes this group of people a community is their union in Christ'. Only the gift of faith enables a man to say, as he points to the consecrated bread and wine, the food for the meal: 'this is the body of Christ; what makes this group of people a community is their sharing in the body of Christ'.

But to say that the real presence of Christ in the consecrated bread and wine is a presence to faith is not to say that it is something 'merely subjective'; the real presence of Christ in people is a presence to faith, but this does not reduce its objective reality. I emphasised earlier that if the use of this language, of these words, gestures and objects, is to be, in objective fact, an encounter with the risen Christ, it can only be so because he has ordained that this language shall have this meaning, shall have this reality; it can only be so because, on the night before he suffered, he took bread into his holy and venerable hands, blessed, broke, and said: 'Take and eat, this is my body.'

Moreover, to say that the real presence of Christ in the consecrated bread and wine is a presence to faith is not to say that it is a 'merely spiritual' presence, whatever that would mean. People only become present to each other, communicate with each other, through bodily words and bodily gestures, through a bodily sharing. That fundamental presence of Christ in the community which I began by describing would not be a reality, it would only be an idea, if we did not bodily meet to know each other, to love each other, to serve each other. That presence of Christ in the proclaimed word which I went on to describe would not be a reality, it would only be an idea, if we did not hear the word, with our bodily ears, as it was proclaimed by someone's bodily voice. Similarly, the presence of Christ in the consecrated bread and wine would not be a reality, it would only be an idea, if we did not share, as our bodily food, through bodily eating processes, a food that is Christ bodily present.

One way of describing, in traditional language, the bodiliness of a thing, is to speak of its substantial reality. If this thing which is the bread we use as part of that complex of words and gestures that go to make up the language of our communication in Christ, is not in fact Christ substantially present then, once again, our sharing would not be a sharing in the body of Christ.

Pope Paul, apparently convinced that some catholics were coming to conceive of Christ's presence in the consecrated bread and wine as a 'merely spiritual' or 'merely symbolic' presence, devoted several paragraphs of *Mysterium Fidei* (39 to 45 in CTS ed) to a defence of the bodiliness of this presence. He then went on to say: 'Beneath these appearances Christ is present whole and entire, bodily present too, in his physical "reality", although not in the manner in which bodies are present in *place*' (46).[3] If we conceive of the presence of Christ in the consecrated bread and wine as a 'local' presence, we tear the heart out of sacramental theology. The teaching authority in the Church has always reacted sharply against the idea that Christ is locally present, but it can hardly be denied that many catholics, not helped by the sort of distorted popular theology to which I referred

[3] Cf the excursus at the end of this chapter.

earlier, do conceive of his presence in this way. The story of the child who, after making her first communion, refused an ice-cream because she 'did not want to make Jesus' head cold' is only a bizarre illustration of a widespread malaise.

This distortion has come about through a failure to appreciate that this particular presence of Christ can only be understood in the context in which it comes about and in which it is employed; and that context is a community, in which Christ is really present, who have assembled, in their consciousness of being the body of Christ, to express and to deepen their reality as human community in the love of God through sharing the body of Christ.

It is sometimes suggested that such a contextual approach to the theology of the real presence does not sufficiently safeguard our belief in the permanence of Christ's presence in the consecrated bread and wine. This objection seems to overlook something of central importance: namely that although we, the church, the body of Christ, are most fully the church when we gather to celebrate the eucharist, we do not cease to be the body of Christ between masses. We are, if you like, always 'standing-by' to be assembled in Christ. The permanence of the presence of Christ in the members of his body is what the doctrine of baptismal character is all about. Similarly, once bread has been consecrated for eucharistic communion, it does not cease to be the body of Christ between masses. It is always 'standing-by' to be used in the christian assembly (whether for communicating the sick and other absent members, or as a focus of praise and adoration by people deeply grate-

ful for the last celebration of the eucharist and looking
forward to the next one).

This insistence that the sacramental presence, sign-
presence of Christ, in the form of bread and wine, can
only be understood in the context of his presence in the
believing community, the context of a people who need
a language to express and to deepen their reality, is no
new-fangled theory thought up by modern theologians:
'The cup of blessing,' says St Paul, 'which we bless, is it
not a communion in the blood of Christ? The bread
which we break, is it not a communion in the body of
Christ? Because there is one bread, we who are many
are one body, for we all partake of the one bread ... just
as the body is one and has many members, and all the
members of the body, though many, are one body, so it
is with Christ. For by one Spirit we were all baptised
into one body—Jews or Greeks, slaves or free—and all
were made to drink of one Spirit' (1 Cor 10.16–17;
12.12–13).

If the celebration of the eucharist is the fullest sacramental achievement of the church, the body of Christ;
if the form this celebration takes is the sharing of a
sacred meal; then the food we share must, in objective
fact, be a food adequate to the reality of the assembly.
The assembly is the body of Christ, really and truly (and
not 'merely symbolically') present in human community.
The only food adequate to this assembly is the body of
Christ, really, truly and substantially present in the
form of food.

The church in the world
We have now briefly considered three modes of Christ's
6+

presence in the eucharist: his presence in the gathered community, his presence in the word proclaimed, and his presence in the food shared. I said at the beginning that I wanted to indicate how a shift in our understanding of the eucharist leads to a corresponding shift in our understanding of the society in which we live. Before doing so it is necessary to outline the relationship of the church, the eucharistic community, to the world as a whole. •

The first point to be made is that the death and resurrection of Christ is the redemptive event for the whole world: there is only one process of redemption. The death and resurrection of Christ is the founding of the kingdom of God. This kingdom, which consists in the achievement of human community in the knowledge and love of God, will only be a completed reality at the end of history: it is what the end of history means. But, between Easter and the second coming of Christ, the redemptive process is at work. What is the function, in this time between, of the church on earth? It is, according to the teaching of the Vatican Council, to be the sign of the kingdom; the sign that God has founded his kingdom in a past event, the sign that God is continuing to bring about his kingdom through all the present vicissitudes of human history, the sign of promise that God will bring his kingdom to its successful future achievement. The church is not an empty, dead sign: she is a living, effective sign, a sacrament. This is why the opening article of the *Constitution on the Church* says that the church 'exists in Christ as the sacrament or instrumental sign of intimate union with God and of unity for the whole human race'.

I said earlier that, considering the sacraments as a form of language, we can distinguish between the terms used, and the meaning the terms have in this language, a meaning given to them by Christ. For my present purpose, I should like to rephrase that slightly, and say that we can distinguish, in the sacraments, the sign and the reality for which the sign exists. The reality is renewed human community in the Spirit of the risen Christ. The sign is the visible society of believers, who hear the word proclaimed and who assemble to celebrate the eucharist. The infallibility of the church means that God will not allow the sign of the kingdom to disappear; there will always be a visible society of believers, the word will always be proclaimed, the eucharist will always be celebrated. But, unless the language is going to be meaningless, the infallibility of the church also entails that to some extent the sign will be effective; that the society of the church will show forth, in its quality of life, that renewed human community for which it exists.

The importance of stressing that Christ died and rose again for all men is that, although the limits of the church at the level of sign can be drawn with some degree of accuracy (I say 'some' degree, because most of the major ecumenical problems arise in this area), it is far less easy to set limits to the existence, at any given moment, of the reality for which the sign exists, the reality of renewed human community (cf arts 14–16 of the *Constitution on the Church*). We must say, however, unless we are to commit ourselves to a totally untenable theory of two processes of redemption, that wherever this reality exists, there is the risen Christ effectively present in his Spirit and, therefore, there in some sense is the church.

Our relationships with other people are by no means limited to our relationships with our fellow catholics, or even our fellow christians. Although our relationships can only be expressed and deepened eucharistically in a certain direction (in conjunction with our fellow catholics or, in certain special circumstances, with our other fellow christians), if we really believe in the universality of the redemption event in Christ, then all our relationships, every form of human community, cries out for eucharistic expression. And the fact that it cannot attain this expression (until the king's great supper of the kingdom), should be a principal source of pain, challenge, and longing, for the christian in the world.

If there is only one redemptive process, then the church and the world are not totally distinct realities, existing in watertight compartments. The church is an aspect of the world, and it is by no means always easy to delineate that aspect. This is only another way of saying that, if there is only one redemptive process, then the history of the church and the history of the world are not totally distinct realities, existing in watertight compartments. The history of the church is an aspect of the history of the world, because the whole history of the world is the history of salvation. God has 'distinguished this particular part of the history from the rest of history and has made it the actual, official and explicit history of salvation'.[4]

[4] Karl Rahner *Theological Investigations* v (London 1966) 106.

The presence of Christ in the world

In the light of such an interpretation of the relationship of church to world, what are the implications, for our general situation, of the threefold analysis of Christ's presence which I earlier discussed in relation to the celebration of the eucharist? If I restrict myself to very broad statements of principle, this is not because I am opposed to the drawing of detailed and concrete conclusions. It is partly because I do not feel myself competent to do more, and partly because there is a very real danger, in drawing concrete conclusions too swiftly from an insight into one aspect of the christian mystery, that one will distort that mystery by overlooking other, and equally fundamental aspects. At a period when all of us in the church are attempting the sort of breakthrough which Bernard Lonergan would describe as the 'shift to a higher viewpoint', there is a need for caution (and not all caution is identifiable with pusillanimity).

1 *In all brotherhood*

In discussing the presence of Christ in the gathered community, I said that the work of our redemption, the work of building human community in the love of God, pre-exists the recognition and acceptance of it by the individual. We are called to renewed community by God, through Christ, in the Spirit. Now, although this fact of being-gathered, this fact that the call of God to brotherhood pre-exists our recognition and acceptance of it, is most fully verified, in sacramental terms, in the eucharistic assembly, this primacy of God's call cannot only be verified there. To claim that it were, would be to deny that God calls all men to the brotherhood of the kingdom. In other words, wherever the christian recognises human brotherhood, however 'secular' or 'non-religious' its form, he necessarily recognises the presence of Christ in the Spirit. Correlatively, wherever the christian recognises the denial of human brotherhood, whether in individual attitudes and activities, or in social, political and economic structures, he recognises the denial of Christ, the presence of the 'world' in the dark, condemnatory sense in which St John usually uses the term. It follows from this that wherever the christian recognises the presence of Christ in the Spirit, he recognises the authoritative demand of the saving God that he demonstrate his solidarity in this brotherhood. But it also follows from this that wherever the christian recognises the denial of Christ in social, political or economic divisiveness, he recognises the authoritative demand of the saving God that he protest, in the name of Christ, against this denial. And since his protest, if it is not to be sterile, cannot be restricted to withdrawal or merely verbal disapproval, it will usually be the case that only through his involvement in the forces that are building brotherhood will he be able to exercise his responsibility of protest against the forces of denial. And because the church on earth, the sacramental sign of the future kingdom, only to a very imperfect degree succeeds in actualising the reality, it will often be the case that his simultaneous affirmation and denial will cut right across the borders of denominational allegiance. The situation will occasionally be clear. If a catholic finds himself a member of a local catholic community which refuses to allow white and coloured people to worship together in the eucharistic assembly, then it is fairly clear that he has a responsibility to join forces with local organisations which are fighting against racial discrimination, however 'secular' their forms or origins.

But the situation, even locally (let alone internationally), will often be far less clear than this. The contemporary social, cultural and political transformation of the world is immensely complex. There can be no excuse for the christian systematically opting out because 'it is all so difficult and the experts probably know best', but it does seem that the courage to see, judge and act needs to include the courage to listen, to be often undecided as to where love lies, and to go on listening. The 'Lord of the Flies' lives in each of us, in every individual and in every pattern of relationships; carrying the cross of Christ includes the very real pain of being unable to distinguish, in the dark, between wheat and cockle, before the daylight of the kingdom comes.

In view of its importance in current theological debate, I can hardly conclude this section without a glance at the question of violence. For centuries christians seemed not to find it queer to praise God, pass the ammunition and turn the enemy's other cheek. It seems ironic that a mood of revulsion against this legacy should go hand-in-hand with a preparedness to employ violent means to bring about that rapid change of social structures which the building of brotherhood demands of us today. Certainly the christian must be prepared to undergo violence for the sake of the kingdom. But is not the decision to inflict violence a decision against universal brotherhood, a declaration of unbelief in the victory of Christ, a human attempt to perform that act of liberation which only God's love can effect, a rationalising denial of the fundamental folly of the cross? It must be admitted that there are plenty of situations in which, because violence is already being inflicted on people (even if 'silently', and without bloodshed), the christian response must itself take a 'violent' form. But to say that violence is thus sometimes morally permissible (and therefore possibly obligatory) is not, I suggest, to deny the principle I am concerned to assert. It is, surely, simply to declare the tragic paradox of man; to declare that, in the concrete, 'perfect love' is frequently not an available option. I should like to see the moral theologians examine some of these situations in the light of their general principle that there always is a 'good' course of action open (some of their attempts to do so, such as the employment of the principle of 'doubt effect', often seem to evade, rather than to embrace, the tragic paradox). Is it not the case that 'the best we can do' (and that we must do) is often pretty poor, and that we would do better to admit the fact in sorrow and anguish, rather than to pretend, by means of abstract principles wielded with ingenious subtlety, that our hands are clean?

2 *In all truth*

In discussing the presence of Christ in the word proclaimed. I said that the fullest realisation of Christ's real presence as word, as declaration of love, is the proclamation of the scriptures in the eucharistic assembly. But Christ, the word made flesh, is truth. Not 'something true', not some partial aspect of truth, but the human manifestation of the very truth, the total truth of God. Therefore, although the proclamation of the scriptures in the eucharist may be the primary verbal articulation of that truth which is Christ, it cannot be the only articulation. To claim that it were would be to deny that God is the source of all truth. In other words, wherever the christian recognises truth, he necessarily recognises the presence of Christ in the Spirit. Correlatively, wherever the christian recognises the denial of truth, he recognises the denial of Christ. Therefore, as in the previous case, the christian will recognise in the presence or absence of truth, the authoritative demand of the saving God to either affirmation or protest in the name of Christ.

The problem of the discernment of truth, and the problem of authority, are one and the same problem. Some of the difficulties we all currently experience in this field are due to false or inadequate statements of the question. But even when the problem of authority is stated with the greatest accuracy and clarity, it remains a problem. To deny that this is the case is either to have failed to see the point, or to have sold out on one's personal integrity. And if a man sells out, it matters little whether he does so in the direction of Eichmann or in the direction of the private hell of personal infallibility.

It is important to bear in mind that the search for the presence of Christ in all truth is far wider than an examination of merely verbal statements. I said earlier that 'the teaching of the church' is, basically, the church herself, as the sign of renewed community; and that the verbal proclamation of the message is only the articulation of the community's self-consciousness, of the community's reality. In other words, when I say that

6*

wherever the christian recognises truth, he necessarily recognises the presence of Christ, I am not referring exclusively, or even primarily, to the recognition of certain statements as true, but rather to the recognition of true living, of human brotherhood. And so this section covers the same ground as the previous one, from a slightly different point of view.

Considerable damage has been done by people behaving as if 'orthodoxy' consisted exclusively in the affirmation of certain propositions as true, and 'unorthodoxy' in the denial of these propositions. If this were the case, then most catholics would undoubtedly be orthodox, and most other people would undoubtedly be not. And yet, an honest examination of the current structures of the church in the light of the new testament, an honest examination of the relationships, attitudes and understanding of catholics in the light of the new testament, suggest that things are not quite so straightforward. This suspicion amounts to certainty when we notice that many people who 'say all the wrong things', so far as verbal orthodoxy is concerned, nevertheless manifest, in their effective concern for human brotherhood, an understanding of the human task which seems far closer to new testament orthodoxy.

In brief, if the relationship between right living and right speaking is that the latter should be the expression of the former, then not only is it inadequate to identify the proclamation of Christ's truth with right statement, but also our search for the real presence of Christ in the word proclaimed in the world will be primarily a search for signs of right living, and only secondarily a search for correct statements. In our fight for the preservation and the realisation of the unchanging truth of Christ, we shall not think we have won the battle when we persuade other people, or ourselves, to talk in a certain way. I shall, of course, have been seriously misunderstood if I have given the impression that the correct articulation in words of the living reality of Christ's truth does not matter.

3 *In all sharing of things*

In discussing the presence of Christ in the food shared, I said that the only food adequate to that assembly which is the fullest sacramental expression of the church, the body of Christ, is the body of Christ, really, truly, and substantially present in the form of food.

But although the sacramental presence of Christ in the eucharistic bread and wine is the fullest presence of Christ in 'a thing shared', it cannot be the only such presence. To claim that it were, would be to claim that the only form of human brotherhood in which Christ is present is the eucharistic assembly. The reason for this is that human brotherhood is always achieved and expressed in the sharing of things. This sharing of things is not something peripheral and unimportant to human community: it is an integral part of the language of human community. To think otherwise is to have a very 'angelic', disembodied view of human nature.

We have already seen that Christ is present, in some way, in all human brotherhood. Therefore we must say that Christ is present, in some way, in all human sharing. Therefore we must say that Christ is present, in some way, in all the things we share. The kingdom of God will consist in a 'new heaven and a new earth';

the Lord of history is the Lord of the world; the word made flesh is the creating word, the ground of meaning for all creation, not only for human beings. Therefore, wherever the christian recognises that things are being used (and this is a general statement about economics) for sharing by people, he recognises the presence of Christ. Correlatively, wherever the christian recognises that things are being used in such a way as formally to exclude somebody, anybody, from the sharing, he recognises a denial of Christ. Perhaps the current attempts in the church to work out a 'theology of poverty', a theology of the presence of Christ in the starving man, the oppressed man, the enslaved man, would do well to include a consideration of this sort. That cup of cold water is not without sacramental significance.

I have been concerned with the presence of Christ in the eucharist. Therefore I used as my text article 7 of the *Constitution on the Liturgy*, with its affirmation of Christ's real presence in the people gathered to form the eucharistic assembly, in the word proclaimed in that assembly, in the food shared by that assembly. I have tried to show that, if we take seriously the fact that the church in the world, and especially the eucharist, is the sacrament of the kingdom, the sacrament of renewed human community in the love of God, then our understanding of, and our participation in this assembly has profound implications for our recognition of the presence of Christ in all brotherhood, in all truth, in all sharing of things. The *Constitution on the Liturgy* is not indulging in empty rhetoric when it says, in article 10, that 'the liturgy is the summit towards which the activity of the church is directed, and the source from which all her power flows'.

Excursus: signs and symbols

It is agreed by all theologians that the presence of Christ in the eucharist is a sacramental presence, and therefore a presence *in genere signi*, in the sign-order. But is the concept of sign-presence sufficient on its own to express the reality of Christ's presence in the eucharist and, in particular, his presence in the consecrated bread and wine? An affirmative answer, such as is implied in my discussion of 'presence' in the two previous chapters, may seem to some people to be inadequate, especially in view of the treatment of the problem in *Mysterium Fidei*. I have therefore thought it helpful to add a comment which I originally drafted (in collaboration with Dom Sebastian Moore) on the encyclical's first appearance. I have not altered the neo-scholastic terminology in which we formulated the distinction I am concerned to make because, for those accustomed to using this somewhat esoteric language, it has the not inconsiderable advantage of precision, thus minimising the chances of being misunderstood. A similar distinction has recently been made, in far greater detail, in an article by Schoonenberg.[5]

The heart of the encyclical, so far as the precise problem of the real presence is concerned, is § 11,[6] where we read:

Nor is it right . . . to be so preoccupied with consider-

[5] P. Schoonenberg, 'Transubstantiation: How far is this Doctrine Historically Determined?' *Concilium* iv, 3 (1967) 41–7.

[6] In the numbering of the cts edition.

ing the nature of the sacramental sign that the impression is created that the symbolism—and no-one denies its existence in the most holy eucharist—expresses and exhausts the whole meaning of Christ's presence in this sacrament.[7]

1. It would seem that this sentence is trying to say that there is an underlying reality in the eucharist that one does not adequately account for by employing the categories of sign and symbol. However, the terms *symbol, sign,* and *sacrament* are convertible to the extent, and only to the extent, to which they refer to a mode of being, reality-as-signifying, which is contradistinguished from other formalities under which reality may be considered.

It is to be noticed that the first half of the sentence recognises this convertibility: '. . . rationi signi sacramentalis considerandae ita instare quasi symbolismus. . . .' However, if one applies this convertibility throughout the sentence, a difficulty emerges:

It is not allowable . . . so to insist on the aspect (*rationi considerandae*) of efficaciously-significant sign as if the sign-quality which all certainly admit in the most holy eucharist expresses fully and exhausts the *ratio* of Christ's presence in this efficacious sign.[8]

---

[7] The latin text is: 'Non enim fas est . . . rationi signi sacramentalis considerandae ita instare quasi symbolismus, qui nullo diffitente Sanctissimae Eucharistiae certissime inest, totam exprimat et exhauriat rationem presentiae Christi in hoc Sacramento'.

[8] Having already given the latin text, and the CTS translation, I have here followed a translation of my own, designed to bring out more clearly the point under discussion.

2. It would seem from the foregoing that the consecrated species, as well as being an efficacious sign of Christ's presence, also contain Christ present in some other manner.

However, if this is the case, then the efficacious sign of Christ's presence does not achieve this other presence of Christ. It can only denote it, point to it, indicate it, as a flag denotes the presence of an unexploded bomb. How is this other presence of Christ achieved, and what is its relation to the efficacious sign which does not achieve it?

3. It could be suggested that the appearances of bread and wine are the efficacious sign, and that this other mode of presence is our Lord's substantial presence underlying the appearances of bread and wine.

This suggestion entails a category mistake. Substantial presence is contradistinguished from accidental presence. Presence-in-sign is, as was suggested in 1, contradistinguished from presence in any other formality under which reality may be considered. In other words, *sign* (efficacious or otherwise) denotes a mode of being, while *substance* and *accident* both denote principles of being. So, for example, it would be a mistake to say: 'This flag is not a sign, it is red' (a category mistake, erroneously contradistinguishing the accident *red* from the formality *reality-as-sign*). Similarly, it would be a mistake to say: 'Jesus of Nazareth is not the sign of God's redeeming love, he is a man' (a category mistake, erroneously contradistinguishing the substance *man* from the formality *reality-as-sign*). The analogy with the eucharistic presence may become clearer if we now rephrase that: 'Jesus of Nazareth is not only the efficacious sign of God's redeeming love, he is also (ie in addition) a man.' This is clearly a muddle: the concept of efficacious sign does wholly express the *ratio* of God's presence in this man.

4. To sum up:

Question: In the blessed sacrament, is Christ present really or sacramentally?
Answer: This is a false question.

Question: In the blessed sacrament, is Christ present accidentally or substantially?
Answer: Substantially; it is this that makes the blessed sacrament unique.

Once the first question is rejected, and the second question is answered as above, then the concept *sacramental sign* does express fully and exhaust the *ratio* of Christ's presence in the blessed sacrament, precisely because it says how Christ is substantially present.

Considerable advances have been made in recent years in our understanding of reality-as-symbolic, reality-as-sign. These advances have made possible a fruitful renewal in christology (Jesus of Nazareth as the Father's word to mankind), in the theology of the church (the church as the 'sacrament or instrumental sign of union with God and of unity for the whole human race'), and in the theology of the sacraments. To this mainstream of contemporary theology the encyclical is not, in the light of the foregoing analysis, directed. As I see it, however, a theologian would not escape the encyclical's censure if, holding a lockeian view of substance and maintaining that all signs merely denote and can never effect presence, he nevertheless affirmed that signification did 'express and exhaust the whole *ratio* of Christ's presence in this sacrament'.

6
Priesthood, ministry, and intercommunion

At a period when the dominant concern of christian thinkers is to understand afresh the very meaning of christianity in terms of our contemporary situation, to grasp the significance of the church and her relationship to the present world and the future kingdom, there is an element of paradox in the fact that questions concerning the place of the ordained ministry in the church should loom as large as they currently do in theological discussion.

These questions seem primarily to arise in two rather different contexts. On the one hand, ecumenical endeavour often meets its stiffest obstacles in this area (as the union in South India found some years ago, and as the anglican-methodist conversations are finding today). On the other hand, within the catholic church, a lively search for fresh understanding of the meaning, role, and mission of the whole people of God is leading to a profound questioning of many aspects of the received theology of the ordained ministry.[1] In other words, a certain preoccupation with the theology of the ministry is not an escape from, but an essential element in, the wider theological search.

It is impossible to discuss the ministry without involving oneself in discussion of basic questions in soteriology, ecclesiology, and the theology of the sacraments. For that reason, a number of central and sometimes controversial issues are touched on in this chapter, without it being possible either to discuss them in detail or adequately to justify the position adopted in regard to them. My aim, however, is a very limited one: to offer a general framework within which, so it seems to me, some important questions may profitably be discussed.

After some remarks about the meaning of christian priesthood and sacrifice, I shall say something about the nature of christian ministry, and about the apostolicity of the church and her ministry. Finally, because of its ecumenical importance and close dependence on the whole question of priesthood, I shall suggest an approach to the problem of intercommunion. The constitutions and decrees of the second Vatican Council form the background to the discussion. They do, however, remain for the most part in the background; the function of a general council is to declare the mind of the church as a whole, not to enter into detailed theological disputes. Nevertheless, it is my belief that the approach adopted is in harmony with the drift of the council's teaching.

[1] Cf (for example) Terry Eagleton, 'Priesthood and Paternalism', *New Blackfriars* xlvii (1965) 141–57; and my own 'The Place of the Priesthood', some comments on Eagleton's article, in *New Blackfriars* xlvii (1966) 564–71.

Priesthood

The popular idea of 'priesthood' in this country is probably reflected fairly accurately by the definition in the *Pocket Oxford Dictionary*, 'a minister of religious worship, an ecclesiastic'. If an opinion poll were conducted on the nature and function of priesthood, it seems likely that the majority of the answers given would be in terms of a class of people set apart for the performance of ceremonial activities in specifically religious buildings. In other words, the ordinary Englishman's idea of a priest is similar to that employed in most primitive religions.[2]

A radical separation of the cultic officials from the rest of the community (implying a strong doctrine of the vicarious nature of official cultic activity) is, however, to some extent dependent upon a magical attitude towards ritual worship. The novel element in old testament worship did not consist in particular forms of religious activity,[3] but in an understanding of ritual worship, not as magic, but rather as the expression of a personal covenant-relationship between God and his people. Therefore although, in Israel, there were cultic

[2] Cf 'The Priest, Pagan and Christian', by P. Idiart, and 'How Christians Regard the Priest Today', by F. Boulard; both in *The Sacrament of Holy Orders* (London 1962), the English translation of papers from a session of the *Centre de Pastorale Liturgique*, held at Vanves, 1955.

[3] 'We know today that there is scarcely a sacrificial concept or practice in the old testament that was not taken over from the Canaanite inhabitants' (H-J. Kraus *Worship in Israel* Oxford 1966, 113). Kraus' whole approach, following Van der Leeuw, to the question of sacrifice (cf 112–24) would lead me to suppose that he would find the broad definition offered in the next paragraph satisfactory.

officials with particular tasks to perform, these tasks were no longer 'merely ritual', but were also, and in some instances primarily, 'prophetic'. That is to say, their function was to bring the worshipping people into an ever renewed and deepened personal relationship with the personal God of the covenant.[4]

The new testament applies the concepts of priesthood and sacrifice to the person and work of Christ.[5] The propriety of this application cannot, however, be regarded as self-evident, in view of the fact that the transformation of the human condition effected in Christ is unique, radical, and total, and therefore transcends all the available categories of human activity. The application becomes even more problematic when, as is often the case, sacrifice is defined in terms of a particular form of religious activity.[6] The fact that, in the face of extremely complex data, such an approach gives rise to as many definitions of sacrifice as there are authors,[7] is hardly surprising, but it may be taken as an indication that the basis for a working definition of sacrifice is perhaps to be sought elsewhere than in comparative ritual mor-

[4] On the prophetic aspect of old testament priestly ministry, cf Kraus, 101–12.

[5] Throughout this chapter, it will be taken for granted that 'Biblically speaking, the idea of priesthood is bound up with sacrifice' (Y. Congar *Lay People in the Church* London 1965, 153).

[6] Cf for example L. Bouyer *Rite and Man* (London 1963) 78–89.

[7] Contrast Bouyer's definition (82): 'what we call by the Latin word "sacrifice" is nothing else than a sacred meal', with that offered by R. de Vaux: 'sacrifice is any offering, animal or vegetable, which is wholly or partially destroyed upon an altar as a token of homage to God' (*Ancient Israel* London 1961, 415. Cf whole section, 415–56).

phology. The simplest and most satisfactory approach seems to be to define sacrifice in terms not of a particular type of activity but of the significance which a particular activity carries within a given society or culture. From this point of view, it seems reasonable to say that any action whose meaning or purpose is an attempted, achieved, or expressed sharing of the divine life by man, may appropriately be described as a sacrifice.[8]

On the basis of an approach such as this to the question of sacrifice, the corresponding notion of priesthood would have no direct reference to consecration for a specific function, to being 'set apart', but would rather be defined as 'the quality which enables a man to come before God to gain his grace, and therefore fellowship with him, by offering up a sacrifice acceptable to him.[9] Whether or not it is appropriate also to describe a priest, thus defined, as a mediator, will depend upon the precise sense with which that somewhat slippery term is employed.[10] In a world without sin, a world in which all human activity adequately expressed full fellowship

[8] Using language as an analogy for human activity in general, this is to say that 'sacrifice' does not denote a particular term or set of terms, but a particular meaning. Alternatively, using the language of classical sacramental theology, we could say that what makes it appropriate to apply the term 'sacrifice' to two different actions is not so much a similarity at the level of *sacramentum*, but rather at that of the *res sacramenti*. Cf above 53–5.

[9] Y. Congar, 154–5, where the author claims that such a definition is necessary 'in faithfulness to Holy Scripture and sound theology'.

[10] One recent study of priesthood suggests that the term 'mediator' is currently employed in three different senses: 'La première situe l'intermédiaire à mi-chemin entre les deux termes à relier, et on comprend qu'il doive être separé (ainsi voyait-on la situation des anges dans l'Ancien Testament). La deuxième imagine l'intermédiaire comme apparenté à l'un et l'autre terme

with God, ritual sacrifice would be unnecessary.[11] All human activity would be sacrificial, and the whole human race would be a priestly people: there would be no men 'set apart'. But, given the fact of sin, mankind's secular activity cannot adequately express a harmony and a sharing which does not exist. Because, therefore, their ordinary human activity cannot show forth a fellowship with God which does not exist, men concoct, in fear and trembling, a 'special' sort of action, the ritual action of symbol and cult. Because the ordinary life of sinful man is not liturgy, he has to create a liturgy which is not ordinary life. Moreover, his fear of God, his sense of distance from God, leads him to set apart special people to handle the business of worship, of attempted commerce with God.

(ainsi Jésus-Christ qui est Dieu et homme). La troisième s'en tient à l'idée de lien: qui alors n'est pas médiateur des lors qu'il contribue à rapprocher les hommes de Dieu, du Christ, de l'Eglise?' (*Qu'est-ce qu'un prêtre?*, by R. Salaün and E. Marcus, Paris 1965, 61).

[11] To speak of a 'world without sin' is not necessarily to make a hypothetical statement about a 'state of pure nature'. On the contrary, writing within the concrete perspectives of salvation-history it is, if anything, to make an eschatological statement. To say this is not to prejudge the value of speculation about 'pre-lapsarian man': it is simply to state that he is not the subject of discussion. Such an approach seems entirely proper in view of the fact that an increasing number of theologians seem to be agreed that the distinction between 'sacred' and 'secular', or between 'religion' and 'life', is only relevant in a sinful world which has, moreover, become to some extent conscious of its sinfulness. This remains true whether one prefers to speak of the process of our redemption in Christ (in which process these distinctions are healed) as the 'sacralisation of the secular' (*consecratio mundi*) or as the 'secularisation of the sacred' (the exorcism of 'religion', the death of the gods).

But Jesus Christ is man without sin, he is the incarnate Son of God. He is, therefore, capable of expressing, in his ordinary life, the relationship that should exist between God and man. And because he is thus the man capable of perfect worship, he does not need ritual actions.[12] His ordinary life is liturgy, and the liturgy which he celebrates is his ordinary life. For him, uniquely, priesthood is exercised in the whole range of ordinary living—and, above all, of ordinary dying: it is difficult to imagine anything less ceremonial, less 'religious', than Calvary.[13]

What are the implications of this radical transforma-

[12] Christ's intrinsic sinlessness, and his total involvement in the 'body of our death' are the poles of a paradox which is only avoided at the cost of making the work of our redemption a 'merely moral', extrinsic, and non-historical affair (cf 2 Cor 5.21; Phil 2.5–11). The style of Christ's earthly life necessarily reflected (eg in his observance of jewish religious practices) that fatal divorce between 'sacred' and 'secular' which he came to heal (cf note 11). In the paschal mystery, this breach between sacred and secular is healed and, in the risen Christ and in his Father's kingdom, they become identical. The church on earth lives in the 'time between', the time in which our 'secularity' is not fully reborn in God, and our 'religiosity' is a witness to the non-achievement of the kingdom (cf the section 'Le culte nouveau', in *Qu'est-ce qu'un prêtre?* 100–12, especially 104).

[13] It is not unimportant to notice that, from the point of view of old testament cultic activity, Jesus Christ was a layman. It is not for nothing that the Letter to the Hebrews, for which the priesthood of Christ is so central a theme, takes great pains not to connect it with the levitical priesthood, but rather with that of Melchizedek: 'So our Lord, of whom these things were said, belonged to a different tribe, the members of which have never done service at the altar' (Heb 7.13). On the relationship between the priesthood of Christ and old testament priesthood, cf the interesting discussion recorded in *The Sacrament of Orders* 44–59.

tion of priesthood and sacrifice for the life of the church? The very existence of the new people of God is the deployment, in the Spirit, of the death and resurrection of Christ, of the perfect sacrifice of Christ the perfect priest. Therefore this people is a priestly people, from the very fact that it draws all its reality from the priesthood of Christ. Therefore the ordinary, secular life of this people is an exercise of priesthood.[14] That is the first point.

The second point is that the faith which brings this people into existence is a response to the preached word, the proclaimed gospel. And so we find, within the people, that group of men whose function it is to convoke the people by proclaiming the word, continually to deepen that people's faith in response to the word, and authoritatively to guide the people in their life according to the word.

If that were the end of the story, we should find ourselves affirming the doctrine of the priesthood of all believers, and of the ministry of the word; but by insisting that this priesthood is exercised in ordinary human activity, we should apparently have excluded all

[14] Cf Rom 12.1. Centuries of clericalism, the demands of post-reformation polemic and a failure to appreciate that the eucharist is the structural focus of the whole life and mission of the church, have combined to obscure this truth of which the fathers were so conscious, and which is reaffirmed in several of the documents of the Vatican Council (cf *Lumen Gentium* 10, 34). 'Now a true sacrifice is every work which is done that we may cleave to God in holy fellowship. . . . Thus man himself, consecrated in the name of God, and dedicated to God, is a sacrifice, in so far as he dies to the world that he may live to God' (St Augustine, in *Civitas Dei*, quoted by Palmer *Sacraments and Worship* London 1957, 282).

ritual and sacramental activity from the life of the christian people.

However, that is not the end of the story. For Christ, ordinary life and liturgy were synonymous. But although we are newborn in the Spirit, although we are, as a people, the visible sign of the kingdom, that kingdom has not yet come. The church is, in her time of pilgrimage, incomplete; she is, and remains, the church of sinners. Therefore our ordinary life, the life of the people on pilgrimage, has not yet attained that perfection which would render symbolic activity irrelevant. Indeed, the very existence of a church which is the sacrament of the kingdom, of a church within a world which is not yet identical with it, bears witness to this fact. The need for a symbolic expression of re-created human community in Christ will only pass away when the whole human race has achieved, by the gift of God, that fullness of brotherhood of which the eucharist, above all, is both the source and the promise.[15]

In other words, to deny the necessity, and indeed the centrality of that sacramental actualisation of the church which is the eucharistic assembly is seriously to over-eschatologise our present situation.[16] But, on the other hand, to claim that sacramental, symbolic activity has the same significance for us as it had for the old people of

[15] If the eucharist is the formal focus in the life of a people whose very nature is sacrificial, then the eucharist must be, in some sense at least, a sacrifice. And if the sacrificial nature of this people is only such in total dependence on, and in participation of, the sacrifice of Christ, the same will be true of the sacrificial nature of the eucharist. Cf chs 2–4, above.

[16] This seems to be, at least at the popular level, one of the principal defects in the current enthusiasm for 'religionless christianity'.

God is to deny the achievement of Christ's victory: is to deny the existence of that deployment of his victory in the Spirit, which is the life of the new humanity in which, by faith, we share.

In brief: for us who share the priesthood of Christ, the sacramental order exists only for the construction of that fulfilled humanity in which, as for its Lord, liturgy and ordinary life will be synonymous.

Ministry

Those general remarks about the common priesthood clearly presuppose a theology of the relationship between creation and redemption, between world and church, whose fuller statement is impossible within the limits of this chapter. They may, however, be a sufficient background against which to introduce some equally general remarks about the ordained ministry. This ministry has already been referred to as 'that group of men whose function it is to convoke the people by proclaiming the word'.[17] I shall assume, without offering proof, that there is, by the Lord's ordinance, an order of ministry in the church, and that this ministry is, in a special sense, a continuation of at least some features of the apostolic ministry.

Is the task of convoking and upbuilding the priestly people of God to be conceived of primarily as a ministry of the word or a ministry of the sacraments? If the christian people is, in its deepest reality, a priestly people, is 'priesthood' the most helpful term with which to characterise the specifically ministerial function?[18]

[17] 175 above.
[18] A central difficulty in trying to ascertain the specific function

It would seem, from the approach adopted in the previous section, that we must say that, fundamentally, christian ministry is a ministry of the word; and a glance at the documents of the Vatican Council seems to support this view. (The Council, of course, recovered a long-lost balance in theology by insisting that the basic form of christian ministry is the episcopate:[19] the presbyterate and the diaconate are only intelligible in dependence on the episcopate). So, for example, the third chapter of the *Constitution on the Church*, after some opening paragraphs on the apostolic office, goes on to say:

> This divine mission, entrusted to the apostles by Christ, is going to last until the end of the world, since the gospel which they have to transmit is the principle of all life for the Church for all time (20).

And, later in the chapter, when the office of bishops is being discussed in detail:

> Outstanding amongst the foremost functions of bishops is the preaching of the gospel (25).

---

of the ordained ministry is that most of the relevant biblical terms apply firstly, and in general, to the church as a whole: apostolic, priestly, prophetic, missionary, and so on.

[19] This is not to prejudge any discussion between episcopal and non-episcopal churches, because the concept of episcopate either held or rejected by the churches is usually based on a superficial theology of the episcopate, and on a preoccupation with secondary, and often questionable, styles of ecclesiastical life and government. It must also be borne in mind that, in the intention of many of the reformers, the office of 'pastor' in the church was to be identified with the episcopate as it existed in the early church, even though the term was usually avoided (cf J. J. von Allmen, 'L'autorité pastorale d'après les Confessions de foi réformés', in *Prophétisme Sacramentel* Neuchatel 1964, 83–107).

Again, in the *Decree on Presbyteral Ministry and Life*:

> It is the word of God which first brings together the
> people of God. . . . Since nobody can be saved without
> faith, the first duty of presbyters as fellow workers
> with the bishops is to preach the gospel to all men (4).

Once again, if there were no more to be said, we should
be forced to conclude that christian ministry is exhaus-
tively described as a preaching ministry, whose function
is to arouse and deepen that saving faith by which men,
in their secular existence, become conscious sharers in
Christ's priestly work of reconciliation.

The previous section should have made clear, however, that there is an important sense in which sacramental activity, and especially the celebration of the
eucharist, is not only necessary for, but is central to, the
wider life and mission of the church.[20] Thus the *Constitution on the Church* says that:

> The bishop . . . is 'the steward of the grace of the high
> priesthood'. This is particularly the case with the
> eucharist, which . . . is the direct source of life and
> growth for the Church (26).[21]

There is, in fact, no contradiction involved in saying
both that the ordained ministry is fundamentally a
ministry of the word, and that it consists centrally in
the presidency of the eucharistic assembly.[22]

[20] Cf *Constitution on the Liturgy* 9–10, and the whole drift of
the argument in 1–2.

[21] Cf *Constitution on the Liturgy* 41, and the *Decree on
Presbyteral Ministry and Life* 5, especially: 'Hence the eucharist
shows itself to be the source and the summit of the whole work
of preaching the gospel.'

[22] Cf Abp Jenny, 'Le Célébrant', in *La Maison-Dieu* LX (1959)

Recent theology, with its reminder that the proclamation of the saving word is a sacramental activity,[23] and that sacraments are words,[24] is helping further to relax this apparent tension. Nevertheless, it is possible to ask the question: is the best term with which to describe the ministerial function, and to describe it as something distinct from the other functions and the general situation of the christian people, the term 'priesthood'? It seems that there is little doubt, on exegetical, historical, and dogmatic grounds, but that the answer is 'no'.[25] In view, however, of the doctrinal implications of the non-use of the term since the reformation, any reluctance to use it now could only give rise to serious misunderstanding. Moreover since christians are increasingly agreed that the Lord Jesus Christ alone is priest in his own

193–212, and J. Lécuyer, 'Le Célébrant. Approfondissement théologique de sa fonction', in *La Maison-Dieu* LXI (1960) 15–29. Daniélou is surely right, so far as methodology is concerned, when he insists that we must 'ask ourselves first what is the purpose of the ministry in the Christian Church', and that it is 'an error of method, in speaking of christian ministry, to approach it first of all through one of its particular aspects, and then to seek to fit it in the others' ('The Priestly Ministry', in *The Sacrament of Orders* 116–17). It is precisely by respecting these methodological requirements that one discovers that primacy of the ministry of the word to which the council documents bear witness.

[23] Cf *Constitution on the Liturgy* 7, and above 82, note 26.

[24] *Verba visibilia*, in Augustine's phrase; cf note 9 above.

[25] It is not by chance that the *Decree on Presbyteral Ministry and Life* prefers the term *presbyter* to *sacerdos* as the general title for the *minister secundi ordinis*; a fact that makes the translation of both terms by 'priest' in the English versions of the decree most unfortunate. I have argued this case in more detail elsewhere: cf 'Priest or Presbyter?', in *Authority in a Changing Church*, London 1968.

right;[26] since christians are increasingly agreed that the ordained ministry is only intelligible within and for the sake of the wider ministry of the church,[27] then we should have little difficulty in agreeing that 'priesthood' is a perfectly proper term with which to describe the ordained ministry, and that its use casts a particular light upon the nature of that ministry. We must, however, ensure that we use the term correctly and not, as we so often have, in a sense that owes more to primitive religion or to the old testament than to christian revelation, and, if a hard-won balance is not to be jeopardised, we must also use the various other terms that have been employed, both in scripture and in the later history of the church, to highlight, each in their own way, the various facets of the mystery of christian ministry.

Having thus outlined a general theory of christian priesthood and of the ministry, it might seem that the next question is: what constitutes authentic ministry, how do we recognise it and how is this sharing in the apostolic office kept alive in the church? This question cannot, however, be answered immediately. If we are convinced that the ordained ministry can only be understood within the church, as a function of the church,[28]

[26] Cf *Constitution on the Liturgy* 7, and the *Constitution on the Church* 10, 60, 62.

[27] 'Bishops rule the particular churches entrusted to them . . . by sacred authority and power, which they only employ for the sake of building up their flock in truth and holiness' (*Constitution on the Church* 27). Cf *Decree on the Pastoral Duties of Bishops* 1; *Decree on Presbyteral Ministry and Life* 1 §2; *Decree on the Missionary Activity of the Church* 2-9.

[28] This point has been made several times because, as a matter of theological method, its importance for our understanding of the church and the sacraments cannot be overestimated. So, for example, if one says that the celebration of the eucharist is central to the life of the church, and therefore central to the function of the ministry, a totally different conception of both

then we have first to ask the question: what constitutes
the church, how do we recognise the church, and how
is the church kept alive in history? In other words, discussion of the apostolicity of the church must precede
discussion of the apostolicity of the ministry.

The churches and the church

The history of the ecumenical movement is, from one
point of view, the history of a deepening recognition of
the fact that the central doctrinal problems to be overcome in the movement towards full unity and authentic
mission are problems in the theology of the church and,
in particular, in the theology of the unity of the church.
Broadly speaking, there are two positions that can be,
and have been adopted in regard to this latter problem.
Both these positions, due to inherent imbalances, tend
to obscure the fact that christian disunity is, doctrin-
ally, a problem at all. Certainly everyone admits that
it is a distressing fact: but not everyone admits that
this distressing fact necessarily involves us in serious
difficulties so far as our understanding of the unity of
Christ's church is concerned. I shall try to summarise
these two positions (and, in doing so, inevitably caricature them).

The first approach, which one associates historically
with Roman catholic theology, takes as its starting-point
the belief that the gifts Christ gave to his church cannot
be lost. Therefore whatever damage is done to the unity

---

church and ministry emerges than would be the case if one said
that the celebration of the eucharist is central to the function of
the ministry, and that therefore the rest of the church has a right
to take part in, to share, the mystery of the eucharistic sacrifice.

of christians through the sins of individuals cannot fundamentally affect the unity of the church. The one church is a visible, sacramental society structured on the belief and organisation given to it by Christ. The Roman catholic christian will say that this fullness of sacramental structure, creed, and church order is to be found in his communion.[29] He will acknowledge that there are many christians, of undoubted sanctity, outside his communion, but their existence will not pose for him serious problems about the unity of the church. It seems important to add that this approach does not necessarily entail either doctrinal arrogance, or an understanding of the goal of ecumenism in terms of 'unconditional surrender'. The gifts we have are gifts to be shared, not to be hoarded or gloated over.

The second approach, which one associates with the theologies of the reformed churches, takes as its starting-point the fact that the promises of Christ will only be fully realised in us at the parousia. Its concern is focused on that saving faith and deepening charity for which sacramental and credal structure exist. There is, it will be maintained, an existing unity of believers in Christ (and therefore an existing unity of the church), the visible manifestation of which, however important, is secondary. There is no difficulty, on this approach, in acknowledging the 'churchness' of other congregations of believers, but their separate existence does not (because of the eschatological emphasis) pose serious problems about the unity of the church. It seems important

[29] It would seem to be the case that this first approach is also broadly that of the orthodox churches, but my ignorance of orthodox theology prevents me from asserting this.

7

to add that this approach does not necessarily entail either an attitude of doctrinal indifferentism or a lack of concern about the importance of ecumenical endeavour.

Both these approaches, in their very different ways, share a common failure to appreciate with sufficient seriousness the problems concerning the unity of the church posed for us by the concrete situation. To try to focus this common weakness more clearly, it may be helpful to employ the categories of classical sacramental theology.

The sacramental order is concerned with the visibility of the grace of God: that God who '. . . saved us and called us of his own purpose and the grace which he . . . now has manifested through the appearing of our Saviour Christ Jesus' (2 Tim 1.9–10). Every sacramental reality, then, consists of a visible element (the sign), and an element of renewed human community in the love of God (the reality for which the sign exists). These two elements are not independent, self-contained realities, but aspects of one reality, the visibility of saving grace; aspects whose mutual relationship may be said to be that between language and meaning.

On such an analysis, the Roman catholic approach to the problem of church unity tends to bypass the problem by concentrating too exclusively on the aspect of sign: of sacramental structure, doctrinal affirmation, church order. The other approach tends to bypass the problem by concentrating too exclusively on the level of grace: of that faith and charity for which the sign exists. But if both sign and grace are essential aspects of that one reality which is the church of God, then look-

ing for that reality in either aspect alone will not provide adequate evidence for answering the question: is
what we have here the church of God?[30]

One useful way of approaching a more satisfactory
statement of the problem is through a discussion of the
relationship between the local and the universal church.
There is a widespread tendency, not confined within the
boundaries of any one denomination, to describe the
local church as a part of the universal church. But there
is an important sense in which the church does not admit
of division into parts and whole. When a group of christians assemble to celebrate the eucharist, they are the
body of Christ sharing in the body of Christ: they are
the church, not a 'part' of the church[31]

> This Church of Christ is truly present in all legiti-
> mate local congregations of the faithful which, united
> with their pastors, are themselves called Churches in
> the New Testament.... In these communities...
> Christ is present, and in virtue of his presence there
> is brought together one, holy, catholic and apostolic
> Church.[32]

[30] Notice how arts 14–16 of the *Constitution on the Church*, in
spite of their dominantly 'structural' emphasis, contain the
crucial assertion: 'Full incorporation in the society of the Church
belongs to those who are in possession of the Holy Spirit...'
(14, cf 1).

[31] 'Through the eucharist we have the whole Christ and not a
"part" of him; and therefore the Church which is actualised in
the eucharist is not a "part" or "member" of the whole, but the
Church of God in her wholeness' (A. Schmemann, 'The Idea of
Primacy in Orthodox Ecclesiology', in *The Primacy of Peter*
London 1963, 38).

[32] *Constitution on the Church* 26. Cf 3, 28, and also *Constitution on the Liturgy* 41.

Any local church, therefore, is the church.[33] The universal church is not some kind of global abstraction, but the family of families, and for each family, each church, one crucial factor in its self-consciousness of its own churchness is its recognition of, and mutual recognition by the other local churches. On the one hand, therefore, where one church recognises the authenticity of another church's eucharistic celebrations, it recognises the church: and if it does so in respect of a body separated from itself, then it necessarily recognises at the same time the existence of divisions in the church. On the other hand, where one church recognises the churchness of another body, it would seem that it necessarily recognises thereby, at least to some extent, the authenticity of its eucharistic celebrations.

An approach such as this to the question of the relationship between the local and the universal church is not undermined by the doctrine of the primacy of the local church of Rome. On the contrary, it is only as 'the fundamental principle of unity of faith and communion',[34] in other words, as the principle of mutual recognition of ecclesial reality, that the unique position of the church of Rome, and of her bishop, becomes in-

[33] 'One plus one is still one in ecclesiology' (N. Afanassieff, 'The Church which Presides in Love', in *The Primacy of Peter* London 1963, 75). For an excellent treatment of the question, by a Roman catholic, cf Gregory Baum, 'The Ecclesial Reality of Other Churches', in *Concilium* IV, 1 (1965) 34–46.

[34] *Constitution on the Church* 18. As a matter of terminology, it seems important to point out that the present writer is not a member of the church of Rome. He is a member of the church of Northampton, whose bishop is in full communion with the bishop of the church (diocese) of Rome.

telligible.[35] Moreover, the assertion that 'This Church (of Christ) . . . subsists in the Catholic Church under the government of Peter's successor and the Bishops in communion with him'[36] must be taken together with the explicit, if necessarily tentative assertion in the *Decree on Ecumenism* that the members of christian communities not in communion with Rome are brought to saving faith and charity in and through those communities (in other words, these communities are not theologically irrelevant agglomerations of individual believers but are, in some sense, churches and, therefore, the church).

We are now in a position to return to the question of the ministry, and to ask: what constitutes authentic ministry, how do we recognise it, and how is this sharing in the apostolic office kept alive in the church?

Authenticity of ministry

It can be assumed, as was said earlier, that there is, by

[35] 'The primacy of the bishop of Rome, therefore, is in no way a monarchical primacy nor does it signify the abolition of the episcopal (and collegial) element—even after 1870. This primacy can be logically understood only in terms of the eucharistic ecclesiology which has just been described' (J. Ratzinger, 'The Ministerial Office and the Unity of the Church', in *JES* I, 1, 1964, 55).

[36] *Constitution on the Church* 8. 'The Church of Christ, then, is realised and embodied in the Catholic Church; conversely, the Catholic Church is the realisation of the Church of Christ on earth, according to Catholic faith the only institutionally perfect realisation of this Church, but there is no simple and unqualified identity. . . . Expressing myself in this careful way, I left room for the complementary aspect which permits me to say that *concretely* and *actually* the Church of Christ may be realised less equally or even more in a Church separated from Rome than in a Church in communion with Rome' (G. Baum, 38, 44, commenting on this article of the *Constitution*).

the Lord's ordinance, an order of ministry in the church. In other words the existence of the ministry is an integral element in the churchness of any community of believers: the ministry pertains to the *esse* and not merely the *bene esse* of the church. Following on from the ideas about the church that have been outlined already, my general answer to the question just raised must therefore be: when one church recognises the ecclesial reality of another body of believers, it thereby necessarily recognises, in some sense, the authenticity of its ministry.

This is a point of crucial importance, which it is necessary to state in very general terms, because it raises further questions which have only recently begun to be discussed, at least among Roman catholics.[37] Historically, one can distinguish two tendencies in the approach to this question of ministry and, not surprisingly, they reflect the emphases and preoccupations that characterise what I earlier described as the catholic and protestant approaches to the question of church unity.[38]

[37] When a new question, or a question that has not previously been raised with sufficient seriousness, arises in theology, one has to begin by employing whatever models are available, even if they do not fit very well. So, for example, Hans Küng raised the question of non-catholic ministry by using the model of 'sacraments *in voto*' (cf *Structures of the Church* London 1965, 184, note 62). More recently, F. J. Van Beeck raised the question by using the model of the 'extraordinary ministry of the sacraments' (cf 'Towards an Ecumenical Understanding of the Sacraments', in *Until He Comes,* Dayton 1968, 141–221). Cardinal Newman made the point succinctly: '. . . a new question needs a new answer', *On the Inspiration of Scripture,* ed J. D. Holmes and R. Murray,(London 1967, 104, note 6).

[38] 'L'Eglise authentique est l'Eglise qui est vraiment apostolique, Comment une Eglise peut-elle être vraiment apostolique

The 'catholic' tendency has been to see the problem of apostolicity as primarily a problem of historical succession. The catholic will only recognise those ministries which can show lineal descent, by imposition of hands, from the apostolic church. Now clearly, if the church is an historical process, if the *traditio verbi in Spiritu* is essentially a fact of history, then this approach contains an important element of truth. It does, however, give rise to some awkward problems. To begin with, it understands apostolic succession as, to use Dr Mascall's image,[39] a sort of relay race: if the baton is dropped, the team in question is permanently disqualified—apostolicity, and so authenticity of ministry, is irretrievably lost.[40]

---

autrement que par succession? Nous arrivons ici au coeur de la question. Il y a diverses manières d'entendre l'expression "succession apostolique". Premièrement, la succession d'évêques designés "ad hoc" pour un siège ou un diocèse: il s'agit ici de succession dans un siège, non de succession par ordination. En deuxième lieu, succession par ordination ou consécration. Enfin, succession dans la travail des Apôtres et dans leur doctrine' (Bernard Lambert *La Problème Oecuménique* Paris 1962, I, 312).

[39] Cf *Corpus Christi* 2nd edition (London 1965) 21–2.

[40] Even in the 'highest' catholic tradition, this approach needs qualifying. As Fr Van Beeck points out: 'Pope Paul VI is *successor Petri*, and not *successor Joannis XXIII*. Historically he comes indeed after Pope John, but he does not formally succeed him: for this a formal transfer of authority would have been requisite' (205). It must also be pointed out that the tendency in recent catholic theology to discuss ministerial apostolicity exclusively in terms of 'valid ordination' does not do justice to other elements in the latin tradition. There were many medieval theologians who, following respectable patristic precedent (which cannot be dismissed simply as being 'donatist' in tendency), denied the possibility of a 'valid' eucharist being celebrated by a dissident minister, however 'valid' his orders. Even St Thomas

A relay race theory of the ministry must, however, entail a relay race theory of the church. If, therefore, a particular community 'unchurches' itself at any point in its history, it can never recover its churchness; and yet current ecumenical developments suggest that few churches would be prepared categorically to declare that such a theory is an integral part of christian doctrine.

A second difficulty can be illustrated by a *casus* of the sort beloved by moral theologians. Imagine a group of people on a satellite, with water, bread, wine, and a radio set—but with no other possible contact with the earth. Through the kerygma proclaimed over the radio they are brought to a fully articulated faith and loving fellowship in Jesus Christ. They use the water to baptise each other (a priestly act of Christ), thus constituting the group as a community sharing in the priesthood of Christ. So far, the case presents no problems. But the time comes when they wish to use the bread and wine to commemorate, with sacramental efficacy, the death of the Lord until he comes. Must we say that their eucharistic assembly in outer space is doomed to be permanently devoid of sacramental authenticity and efficacy? If not, then it must surely be suggested that they are capable of acquiring an authentic ministry, an authentic episcopate, an authentic liturgical presidency (while granting, of course, that the full authenticity of this ministry will depend on its recognition by the earthbound church, the historic episcopate).[41]

---

was prepared to say of such a minister that 'redditus est impotens ad sacrificium offerendum' (*Summa Theologica* III, 8.10 ad 2; quoted by Lécuyer, 26. Also cf Van Beeck on 'antithetical celebrations').

[41] '. . . in view of the extraordinary situation, the bona fides.

The other general approach to the problem of apostolicity is not primarily concerned with historical succession. Its criterion is rather: what goes on, here and now, in a given congregation? What is the doctrine they profess, the life they lead? If the answer is that this congregation authentically images, in doctrine, order, and witness, the blueprint image of the apostolic church, then this is the church of Christ, and is therefore equipped with an authentic ministry.[42]

The chief difficulty with this approach is that it is insufficiently historical. It ignores the fact that the faith once given to the saints, and enshrined in the scriptures, can only be recognised as that unchanging faith within that maintained historical consciousness which we call

---

and the authenticity of the diakonia, supported by the faith and the ecclesial character of the community, the ministry of (the word and) sacraments as exercised by Protestant ministers may in terms of the Roman Catholic church order be qualified as recognizable as an extraordinary ministry' (Van Beeck, 190). The obverse of the tendency (remarked on in note 40) to deny any authenticity to antithetical celebrations, regardless of 'who ordained the minister', must be a tendency to attribute some authenticity to celebrations that are not in fact antithetical (ie are not formally schismatic or heretical), regardless of who ordained the minister.

[42] A rather uncompromising recent example of this tendency is A. Cochrane's study: 'The Mystery of the Continuity of the Church: a Study in Reformed Symbolics', in *JES* II, 2 (1965) 81–96. However, many protestant writers would claim that to discuss ministerial authenticity to the exclusion of any consideration of 'material succession' does not do justice to other elements in the reformed tradition (cf eg 'The Continuity of the Church According to Reformed Teaching', by J. J. Von Allmen, in *JES* I, 3, 1964, 424–44, especially 431, and 'A Protestant View of the Ecclesiological Status of the Roman Catholic Church', by George A. Lindbeck, in *JES* I, 2, 1964, 243–70, especially 251).

the tradition. It does, however, have the merit of stressing the fact that the apostolicity of the church, and of the ministry, is not only a matter of 'handing-on': what is handed on is of equal importance.

It seems clear that these two approaches to the apostolicity of both church and ministry are essentially complementary, and the realisation that this is the case has important consequences for an evaluation, not only of our own ministry, but also for that in the separated churches.

In the first place, the concept of 'validity of orders' is too narrow to form the basis of a judgement concerning the authenticity of the ministry within a particular church. One reason for this is that 'validity' is essentially a canonical concept. The application of the terms *valid* or *invalid* to a particular act of the church is the canonical recognition that this act satisfies, or fails to satisfy, certain theological criteria. What need to be examined, therefore, are the theological criteria according to which a particular ministry or sacrament is, in the concrete, considered to be authentic or defective. The possibility cannot be ruled out a priori that the theological criteria which underpinned a judgement of 'invalidity' in a given case may, at some later period, come to be seen to have been inadequate. In the case of anglican orders, for example, it seems certain that the theological criteria upon which Roman catholic declarations of invalidity have, in the past, rested, entailed the assumption that the ministry could be sufficiently defined in terms of sacrificial function.[43] Since the second Vatican Council,

---

[43] In *Apostolicae Curae*, for example, the weight of the argument bears on the statements: '...ordinem sacerdotii vel eius

with its insistence that the essence of christian ministry consists in the manifold functions of episcopacy (in terms of which the subsidiary offices of the presbyterate and diaconate have then to be defined), it is no longer possible to accept such a definition as adequate. Therefore the question arises: does not a broader understanding of the nature of the ministry entail the realisation that the magisterium has never formally evaluated any but one partial aspect of the anglican ministry?[44]

In the second place, the concept of validity is strictly irrelevant to the prophetic aspect of christian ministry. It is of the essence of the prophetic gift that, although one may be entitled to expect its rich distribution to the men whose foremost official function it is to proclaim God's saving word to his people, nevertheless it is incapable of being 'contained' within canonical structures (with which alone validity is concerned). This consideration raises questions about the light in which we might

---

gratiam, et potestatem, quae praecipue est potestas consecrandi et offerendi verum corpus et sanguinem Domini, eo sacrificio, quod non est nuda commemoratio sacrificii in cruce peracti'; '... in primis episcopatus muniis illud scilicet est, ministros ordinandi in sanctam Eucharistiam et sacrificium ...' (Denzinger 1964, 1965).

[44] To formulate the problem in this way is neither to resolve, nor to deny the interest of the historical dilemma (cf Francis Clark *Eucharistic Sacrifice and the Reformation* London 1960; Anthony Stephenson, 'Two Views of the Mass: Medieval Linguistic Ambiguities', in *Th St* XXII, 1961, 588–609; John Jay Hughes, 'Ministerial Intention in the Administration of the Sacraments', in *Clergy Review* LI, 1966, 763–76; John Jay Hughes, 'Two English Cardinals on Anglican Orders', in *JES* IV, 1967, 1–26); it is simply to suggest that the heart of the matter lies elsewhere.

regard even the least 'sacramentally organised' of the protestant ministries.

In the third place, it would be inconsistent with the approach that has been adopted throughout this chapter to be content with any examination of the ministry within a particular church that was not, firstly, an examination of the church in question. In other words, the question must be asked: could not an examination of the sacramental life, teaching, and church order of a separated christian community result, perhaps, in a clear recognition of its authentic churchness, with a consequent necessary recognition of its ministry (and the legal consequence of such a recognition would be a declaration of validity)?[45] It is, of course, necessary to add that a full recognition of churchness would, in accordance with the theology of the relationship between the local and the universal church which was outlined above, be a mutual business, and would therefore entail, in theory and practice, a recognition on the part of the separated church of the primacy of the church (the diocese) of Rome, and of her bishop. Finally, for the sake of completeness, it must be said that to suggest that such an approach is possible, or even necessary, once the existence of 'ecclesial reality' outside the Roman communion has been admitted, is not to have begun to solve the many intractable detailed problems that stand in our way.

Intercommunion

Any discussion of christian priesthood and ministry

---

[45] It must be borne in mind that, because no church stands exactly where it did five or ten, let alone four hundred years ago, this examination must be a continual process.

must inevitably raise questions concerning the possibility of common worship by members of separated
churches and, in particular, of intercommunion. Such
discussion should take as its starting-point the fact that
the mutual recognition, by all christians, of their common sharing in the priesthood of Christ through bap-
tismally sealed faith, demands that only the most serious
of obstacles can stand in the way of the full expression
of this common priesthood in the celebration of the
eucharist.

At the present time, most of the christian bodies are
convinced that obstacles of sufficient seriousness do exist
insofar as their relationships with most other christian
bodies are concerned. Before saying something about
these obstacles, there are two preliminary points to be
made.

First, by *intercommunion*, I mean at least full open
communion as 'the result of an agreement between
churches'.[46] I leave on one side the question of what is

[46] Leonard Hodgson. His full proposed definition, taken up by
the theological commission reporting to the 1952 Lund conference on faith and order, runs: 'Intercommunion should be
used to mean the result of an agreement between Churches of
different denominations whereby the communicant members of
each may freely communicate at the altars of either . . . there are
also cases in which, without any such agreement between
Churches, a Church may by unilateral action welcome members
of other Churches to share as guests in its Communion Services.
This may conveniently be called "open communion". If two
Churches welcome each other's members, and the members of
both are allowed to accept the open communion is mutual; if
the invitation is only given or taken in one direction, it is one-
sided. . . . Intercommunion and open communion both imply the
existence of separately organised denominational Churches, in
each of which the Sacrament is administered by its own ministers.

meaningful or proper from the point of view of an individual acting apart from, or contrary to the position adopted by the church to which he belongs (this question seems to belong to the moralist rather than to the dogmatic theologian).[47]

Secondly, it is not unimportant to note that the general attitude of the churches towards intercommunion reflects the distinction made earlier in this chapter between a 'catholic' and a 'protestant' understanding of the unity of the church. Thus it is not surprising that the catholic and the orthodox churches, with their stress on the sacramental visibility of grace, should tend to see intercommunion as a goal rather than as a means. Similarly, it is not surprising that those churches whose primary stress is laid upon the faith and charity for which the structural aspects of the mystery of the church

---

If members of other Churches are welcomed by either inter- or open communion, but ministers are not allowed to act as celebrants except in the services of their own Churches, there is not so close a degree of inter-Church unity as where an interchange of ministers would also be permitted. For this freedom of ministers to officiate sacramentally in either Church, the term "intercelebration" is convenient' (*Intercommunion*, ed Donald Baillie and John Marsh, London 1952, 18ff. I have quoted the passage from 'Freedom of Worship: Intercommunion', by Martin Redfern, in *Christians and World Freedom* (London 1966) 49–50.

[47] 'First of all, *communicatio in sacris* may not be an act of indifference or disloyalty towards one's own Church.... Neither for the individual participant nor for a group of participants representing one particular Church may the participation in an interfaith celebration have the character of an antithetical, dissentient gesture directed against his or their church order and creed' (Van Beeck, 217–18).

exist, should tend to see intercommunion as an excellent means towards the goal of full christian unity.[48]

There are two types of obstacle which are usually admitted to stand in the way of intercommunion: those concerning doctrine and those concerning church order. If we admit that some degree of prior agreement on doctrine (not simply eucharistic doctrine, though this would be central) is necessary before intercommunion is even intelligible, the question is: what degree? If one were to say 'complete agreement', I am not sure what this would mean, because there is, for example, a considerable divergence in doctrinal assent between the members of any given congregation of Roman catholics at

[48] It is important to notice that the council's *Decree on Ecumenism* is aware of the importance of both sides of the question: '*Communicatio in sacris*, however, is not to be applied indiscriminately as a means to the reunion of christians. Sharing of this kind is based on two principles: expression of the unity of the Church and sharing in the means of grace. Expression of unity excludes sharing for the most part. The grace to be won sometimes recommends it' (8). So far as the relationship of intercommunion to other forms of common worship is concerned, Fr Van Beeck has a useful remark: 'The traditional distinction between joint prayer and reading of the Word on the one hand, and the joint celebration of sacraments on the other hand, though by no means unreal, must not be exaggerated. Prayer and Bible services are all too often permitted "because nothing happens in them", as if prayer and the Word were not sacramental. On the other hand, there is a tendency to view joint celebration of sacraments as acts of the most perfect *communio* which, therefore, would have to be postponed till the day on which mutual recognition would be achieved. But is this not to forget that the *communio in via* will never be perfect and that it is also in the nature of a sacrament to be a *pledge* of salvation? It seems not wholly sound to consider the sacraments so eschatological as to practically deny that they are a part of the *status viae* of the Church' (216, note 80).

mass on a Sunday morning.[49] So one would have to say 'there must be sufficient agreement'. What precisely would constitute a sufficient agreement cannot possibly be worked out by either of two separated churches unilaterally and a priori. It would have to be an agreement worked out by both parties to be a sufficient agreement (there is an important analogy here with the historical function of credal formulations of faith).

What about church order, by which is meant not only, or even primarily, the assessment of juridical questions of validity and the like, but doctrinal positions in ecclesiology as they find juridical expression? Here, once again, the key should be mutual recognition by churches

[49] It could be objected that such differences are 'merely theological' and not differences in faith. Although the distinction between faith and its formulation is currently acquiring more, not less importance, it can no longer be assumed that the distinction between differences in the formulation of a common faith and differences in faith itself is as easy to locate as it may sometimes have seemed to be. Theology is the articulation of belief. It may well be the case that two people, united in faith, articulate their common belief differently. But it cannot be assumed that mere assent to identical propositions is sufficient evidence of unity in faith. Christian faith is a personal commitment, in the Spirit, to the God and Father of our Lord Jesus Christ. If two people assent verbally to identical creeds, and recognise themselves as bound by a common church order, but each of them gives a merely 'notional' assent to all but one of the articles of the creed, and the one article to which each of them gives a 'real' assent is different in each case, then must we not say that they are divided in faith, and not 'merely in theology'? Whatever the intrinsic connection between the articles of the creed (whether from the point of view of logical entailment or from the point of view of redemptive-historical fact), it can hardly be denied that such situations can, and do exist. (On this whole question cf Charles Davis, 'Unity and Christian Truth', in *The Eastern Churches Quarterly* XVI, 1964, 101–16.)

of their respective churchness and authenticity of ministry. To say that this whole question of the possibility of intercommunion is one that, from the Roman catholic point of view, cannot currently be considered, seems to me to be tantamount to a denial of recognition of any genuinely ecclesial element in other christian bodies. In which case it is hard to reconcile with the clear teaching of the Vatican Council.

It was suggested earlier that, on an integral sacramental theology, the two approaches to the question of church unity were complementary. If, then, it is true that the protestant must take seriously the extent to which sacramental activity is not simply an optional form of prayer for unity on the part of men already united in faith and charity, but is also the sign of an achieved unity (and therefore problematic where structural unity is not yet achieved), it would also seem that, on the other hand, the catholic tradition must take seriously the extent to which the recognition of other christians as christians (a recognition of their truly christian faith and witness) demands sacramental expression. (I prefer not to speak, at any point, of an 'existing invisible unity', because faith and witness are visible realities, even when they have not yet found sacramental and structural expression.)

So far as mutual recognition of ministry is concerned, I have outlined an approach which seems to do justice both to the central importance of the historic episcopate, and to the undoubted existence of effective ministry in the separated churches (both those which do not 'have bishops' and those whose bishops we do not currently recognise).

The danger of too readily accepting intercommunion between separated churches would be that, as we diminished the significance of the eucharist as the expression of a unity already achieved, we would tend to diminish our sense of the urgent need to go on even further: we might become lazily content with less than the Lord demands, because the later stages of the road are bound to become more difficult.

On the other hand, the danger of denying the possibility of all intercommunion before full unity were attained might mean that we should never reach the goal: our refusal might be a refusal to acknowledge sacramentally the extent to which the Lord, and not men, is in fact healing the divisions amongst his people.

There is, however, a third factor which seems to argue for the greatest caution in this matter. Fear, suspicion, ignorance, and mutual cultural and existential isolation are every bit as powerful as the formally theological factors in our divisions. For this reason I am a little uneasy when it is suggested (as several catholic theologians have suggested recently) that intercommunion should be possible, here and now, at least at specifically ecumenical gatherings and conferences. The way to overcome the formally non-theological factors in our divisions is through an ever deeper collaboration in life, work, and witness.[50] Without such a 'growing together' in the concrete, for the church authorities in any denomination to encourage a few people to do something which would be totally unintelligible to the majority, would be to court disaster. Serious disunity within one or more churches seems a high price to pay for the occasional

[50] Cf *Decree on Ecumenism* 12.

sacramental expression of unity amongst the ecumenically alert.[51]

The judgement as to the appropriate policy in this matter depends on the constantly developing concrete situation.[52] My concern in this section has simply been to indicate why it is that the possibility of intercommunion prior to full unity between two churches should not be regarded as out of the question, from the Roman catholic point of view, on either doctrinal grounds or grounds of church order.

Conclusion

It would be encouraging if the approach suggested in this chapter to the questions of priesthood, ministry, and common worship should prove acceptable, not only to catholics, but also to many other christians. Even if this turns out to be the case, none of us have any cause for complacency. Not only do the very general terms of a discussion such as this leave unexplored some of the more intractable theological issues; more important, a 'notional' assent to common doctrine must develop into that 'real' assent which would seek and find vast areas of common service in the world in which and for which we have our mission. Only in this way will the church, the 'sacrament of intimate union with Christ and of unity for the whole human race'[53] come to fulfil, less inadequately, its unique function in the history of the world.

---

[51] 'Communicatio in sacris ... must always take the existing church order into account, also in the sense that it may never give undue scandal to the "ordinary" Church members. Chapters 8–10 of the first Epistle to the Corinthians remain the rule of all conduct, also in these matters' (Van Beeck, 218).

[52] Cf Decree on Ecumenism 8.

[53] Constitution on the Church 1.

Index of Biblical References

Bibliographical Index

The following list includes all the works referred to in this book, together with other books and articles of particular relevance. Where the work listed has been referred to in this book a reference to the page on which it was mentioned has been placed at the end of the entry.

Afanassieff, N. "The Church Which Presides In Love," *The Primacy of Peter*. London, 1963: 186.

von Allmen, J. J. "L'autorité pastorale d'après les confessions de foi reformées," *Prophetisme Sacramental*. Neuchâtel, 1964: 178.

———. "The Continuity of the Church According to Reformed Teaching," *Journal of Ecumenical Studies*, I 3 (1964): 191.

———. *Worship: It's Theology and Practice*. London, 1964.

Audet, J.-P. "Literary Forms and Contents of a Normal Eucharistia in the First Century," *The Gospels Reconsidered*. Oxford, 1960. [This essay first appeared in *Studia Evangelica: Papers Presented to the International Congress on "The Four Gospels in 1957"* (K. Aland *et al*, Eds.). Berlin, 1959, 623–662. In French: *Revue Biblique*, LXV (1958), 371–399]: 77–78, 80–83, 85–86, 88.

Augustine of Hippo. *The City of God*: 56, 175, 180.

———. *Commentary XXVI on the Gospel of John*: 63.

Baillie, D. and Marsh, J. (Eds.). *Intercommunion*. London, 1952: 196.

von Balthasar, H. U. "Personne et fonction," *Parole de Dieu et Sacerdoce*. Tournai, 1962.

Baum, G. "The Ecclesial Reality of Other Churches," *Concilium*, IV 1 (1967): 186–187.

van Beeck, F. J. "Towards an Ecumenical Understanding of the Sacraments," *Until He Comes* (N. Lash, Ed.), Part II. Dayton, 1968: 188–190, 196–197, 201.

Betz, J. "Sacrifice et action de grâces," *La Maison-Dieu*, LXXXVII (1966): 78, 82.

Blenkinsopp, J. "Presbyter to Priest: Ministry in the Early Church," *Worship*, XLI 7 (1967).

Boelens, W. "Eucharistic Developments in the Evangelical Churches," *Concilium*, IV 3 (1967): 125.

Botte, B. "Tradition apostolique et canon romain," *La Maison-Dieu*, LXXXVII (1966): 85.

Boulard, F. "How Christians Regard the Priest Today," *The Sacrament of Holy Orders*. London, 1962: 170.

Bouyer, L. *Eucharistie: Theologie et Spiritualite de la Priere Eucharistique*. Tournai, 1966: 73.

——. *Life and Liturgy*. London, 1962: 101.

——. *Rite and Man*. London, 1963: 50–51, 97, 100, 121, 171.

Chalcedon, Council of, quoted: 3, (19).

Clark, F. *Eucharistic Sacrifice and the Reformation*. London, 1960: 51, 108, 119, 125–127, 129–132, 134–135, 193.

Cochrane, A. "The Mystery of the Continuity of the Church: a Study in Reformed Symbolics," *Journal of Ecumenical Studies*, II 1 (1965): 191.

Colson, J. *Ministre de Jesus-Christ ou le Sacerdoce de L'Evangile*. Paris, 1966.

Congar, Y. *Lay People in the Church*. London, 1963: 171–172.

Cooke, B. "Synoptic Presentation of the Eucharist as Covenant Sacrifice," *Theological Studies*, XXI 1 (1960): 48–49.

——. "Eucharist: Source or Expression of Community," *Worship*, XL 6 (1966).

Cunningham, A., and Eagleton, T. "Community," *Catholics and the Left*. London, 1966: 35.

——. "Politics," *Catholics and the Left*. London, 1966: 36.

Daniélou, J. "The Priestly Ministry," *The Sacrament of Holy Orders*. London, 1962: 180.

Davis, C. "The Danger of Irrelevance," *The Study of Theology*. London, 1962: 37.

——. "Theology and Its Present Task," *Theology and the University* (J. Coulson, Ed.) London, 1964: 37.

——. "Unity and Christian Truth," *The Eastern Churches Quarterly*, XVI (1964): 198.

Denis-Boulet, N.–M. "Notions générales sur la messe," *L'Eglise en Prière*. Tournai, 1961: 78, 98.

Dix, G. *The Shape of the Liturgy*. London, 1945: 105.

Dodd, C. H. *The Apostolic Preaching and Its Development*. London, 1963: 40.